Cryptocurrency Investing

Earn at Least 2K per Month by Investing in Crypto Currencies, Get the Most Out of Trading, NFT, and DeFi

Written by:

Liam McAllen

Table of Contents

Introduction

The cryptocurrency market is volatile and it can be difficult to make wise investment decisions. Cryptocurrencies are based on blockchain technology, which means that there are no central banks managing transactions. There are also no limits on how much you can withdraw, unlike traditional banks.

This makes the crypto market an interesting place for investors, but also uncertain due to its volatility. Before you invest in cryptocurrencies, think about the location where your preferred exchange is based, transaction fees charged by exchanges and other websites, the security of your investments (are they held offline or online), and general market trends (recent news about cryptocurrency, etc.).

Cryptocurrency is decentralized digital money governed in part by blockchain technology and safeguarded by encryption. This means that many different types of cryptocurrencies exist on a blockchain.

Cryptocurrencies are often misrepresented to novice investors, referred to as 'altcoins' where they are typically only worth a few dollars per coin; however, the price of Bitcoin has increased ten-fold in the last decade, plus or minus volatility. Whilst many coins have had fantastic rises in value in recent years, there have also been plenty of crashes that can make it hard for new investors to find the best cryptocurrencies for their investment portfolio.

A cryptocurrency is defined by its algorithm, which is essentially a code that determines how the currency works. The algorithm can be adjusted to enable the currency to be 'mined' or created. The more people who mine it and the greater their investment, the higher its value generally rises over time. Bitcoin for example was created in January 2009 by an unknown person using the alias Satoshi Nakamoto and uses proof of work, which is essentially a variation of blockchain technology. There are currently more than 1600 different cryptocurrencies available, each with its own relevance and method of creation varying.

Many investors see cryptocurrency as a good investment due to its decentralized nature. This means that the value of each unit is not influenced by any bank or government—making it a more reliable investment than traditional fiat currencies such as USD or Sterling.

You can spend cryptocurrencies on various things depending on the cryptocurrency: some are easier to spend, others are only useable at a certain store or group of stores. Ethereum is famous for having the most variety in what you can buy with it, from houses to designer shoes, though you need to dig around online for listings and prices.

Chapter 1. What Are Cryptocurrency and Blockchain?

What Is Cryptocurrency?

Cryptocurrencies are digital currencies that use cryptography for security and verification purposes. These currencies typically use decentralized control with no central authority such as government or financial institution, though there are some centralized cryptocurrencies, like bitcoin. Cryptocurrencies can be traded publicly by anyone in digital wallets using online exchanges and physical cash is sometimes placed directly into digital wallets using paper wallets. Cryptocurrencies are classified as a subset of digital currencies and are also classified as a subset of alternative currencies and virtual currencies.

The first cryptocurrency to be created was Bitcoin in 2009 introduced by an anonymous programmer known as Satoshi Nakamoto. It uses SHA-256 cryptography to secure the network and create new coins, it is also called a proof-of-work system. A few years later, Litecoin was introduced in October 2011. This cryptocurrency uses scrypt to secure the network. Many other cryptocurrencies were introduced after this, with the most popular ones today being Bitcoin Cash, Monero, Ethereum, and Ripple.

These currencies are meant to be used as a medium of exchange, and the private and public keys that go with them are used to transfer value. The most common method of using cryptocurrency is through a mobile app. Users can pay users who have the apps by sending cryptocurrencies to the latter. Cryptocurrencies also have huge potential in cross-border payments as they provide an inexpensive alternative to international wire transfers and other traditional payment services.

For example, imagine that you want to buy something online and you want to pay with bitcoin (BTC), this will be much faster than using a credit card, or right upon buying it you withdraw it in fiat currency for your bank account. This is because you don't need to wait for your payment to go through the bank, credit card company, or PayPal.

Bitcoin, the first-ever cryptocurrency was invented by an anonymous group (or person) known as Satoshi Nakamoto. Bitcoin was released as open-source software to the broader public in 2009. This means that anyone can access it and make their own changes.

Bitcoin is a 'crypto' short for 'cryptocurrency' which uses cryptography and the hash cash proof of work function for the creation of coins and for securing transactions. To safeguard transactions and manage the creation of new coins, cryptography is used. Hash cash is the proof-of-work function that solves the double-spending problem.

There are currently more than 1,000 cryptocurrencies available. The main goal of all cryptocurrencies is to create a decentralized payment system. This means that no one central authority such as a bank controls or issues new units of currency. This also means that individuals or companies cannot issue new units of currency and profit from them without the public's permission, much like with physical cash.

Cryptocurrencies are used primarily outside existing banking and governmental institutions and are exchanged over the Internet. While this alternative, decentralized modes of exchange are in the early stages of development, they have the unique potential to challenge existing systems of currency and payments. As of June 2018, the total market capitalization of cryptocurrencies is bigger than 170 billion USD, and the record high daily volume is larger than 11 billion USD.

Bitcoin is not owned by a particular person or entity like JPMorgan Chase or PayPal but instead exists on the internet independently. It uses blockchain technology to track transactions rather than one entity tracking transactions, which cuts out the middlemen. However, in blockchain technology, digital money is now generated through mining and this mining serves two purposes. First, it creates new Bitcoins at a slow and steady rate which ensures the currency is stable. Second, mining helps confirm transactions on the blockchain. This is the main innovation of Bitcoin over e-gold which used a central server to track balances.

Many cryptocurrencies are designed to be a medium of exchange that uses cryptography to secure transactions and control the creation of new units of cryptocurrency. They are decentralized peer-to-peer currencies. Unlike currencies issued by central banks, there is no central authority to issue new units of these cryptocurrencies (or tokens).

Fiat currencies such as the U.S. dollar, Euro, and Japanese yen are issued by central banks and government agencies. Fiat currencies are created by governments to facilitate trade, as a store of value, and as a unit of account. Central banks issue fiat currencies that are backed by the severe assets of the country. The U.S. dollar, Euro, and Japanese yen, for example, are backed by U.S. Treasury Notes, and the Japanese yen is backed by Japanese government bonds. Because cryptocurrencies are decentralized and not issued or controlled by a single central authority, they are more resistant to restriction as well as being less susceptible to inflation.

What Is Bitcoin?

Just as we can interact with physical currency without the involvement of banks or other centralized institutions, Bitcoin is designed to enable peer-to-peer monetary transactions without trusted intermediaries. You will learn what it is and then how it works later in the chapter.

Let us look at James' example to understand what a typical Bitcoin could do for you. James is a close acquaintance of John. James is 40 years old and lives in the USA. Recently, he has switched his mode of payment to digital currency. According to James, he makes all the significant transactions through Bitcoin. For example, recently, he purchased a sports car with his Bitcoin. James stores his Bitcoin in a specialized Bitcoin wallet, and the money is transferred using only blockchain technology. We will talk about the Blockchain later in this chapter, but let us first see how the Bitcoin transactions have benefited James:

- Bitcoin transactions are discreet. This means that James's identity is not revealed with a Bitcoin transaction, unlike traditional payment methods.

- James has greater autonomy using Bitcoin, as he does not have to deal with banks or the government. He can control how he spends his digital money.

- In addition, James can send payment to anyone on a network worldwide without any external authority's approval. This means Bitcoin provides James with a peer-to-peer transaction system.

- He can make payments with a single click on his mobile phone. In short, James only requires internet access to make payments on his Bitcoin.

- James has avoided banking fees such as overdraft charges and account maintenance fees by utilizing Bitcoin for payments.

After looking at James' case, are you beginning to understand the application of Bitcoin? Do you think there would be any other benefits of Bitcoin?

Bitcoin is a decentralized cryptocurrency that isn't tied to any particular currency and works on a worldwide basis. It is fully decentralized in every way—technical, logical, and political. New Bitcoin is mined as transactions are authenticated, and as already discussed above, a maximum of 21 million Bitcoin will ever be generated. To hit 21 million Bitcoin, it will take approximately until the year 2140. Anyone with enough processing power can engage in Bitcoin mining and help create new Bitcoin. After the total number of Bitcoin is generated, no new coins can be minted; only those already in circulation can be used. Take note that Bitcoin, unlike national fiat currencies, does not have defined denominations. Bitcoin, by default, can have any value with a precision of eight decimal places. Thus, the smallest unit of Bitcoin is 0.00000001 BTC, abbreviated as 1 Satoshi.

Have you ever considered investing in Bitcoin but backed away from that choice due to a limited budget? Then you might need to reconsider your decision. We will look at Eva's scenario to understand Satoshi's concept in a better way. Eva lives in the U.K. and has been curious about Bitcoin for some time now. Once she learned the basics of Bitcoin, she downloaded a wallet to her smartphone and bought some crypto. Eva just learned that like the pound can be divided into pence and U.S. dollar into cents, each Bitcoin could also be divided into the smallest unit known as Satoshi. Each Bitcoin comprises 100 million Satoshis.

Eva also knows that she can purchase Satoshi just as she can get Bitcoin, i.e., through Crypto or online exchanges. She can also use Satoshi cranes, which may provide another way to own cryptocurrency. Eva can keep her Satoshi coins in her Bitcoin wallet in the future.

After some months of learning about Bitcoin, Eva noticed that her 'normal money' did not keep up with Bitcoin's price and could not afford to buy a full Bitcoin. However, much to her delight, Eva was still able to invest in Bitcoin trading. Instead of purchasing the entire Bitcoin that was out of her budget, she purchased it in small fractions. These small fractions are known to be the Satoshis that Eva had already known about during her learning period.

Miners process transactions to create new coins and consume the transaction fee that the party wishing to conduct the transaction is willing to pay. When the total supply of coins exceeds 21 million, miners can verify transactions solely to collect transaction fees. However, suppose anyone attempts to make a transaction without paying a transaction charge. In that case, it will still be mined because the transaction is legitimate (if it is valid at all), and the miner is more interested in the mining incentive that allows him to produce new coins.

Are you curious about how the worth of Bitcoin is determined? When currency was backed by gold, it carried great weight and was easy to value according to gold standards. When we conclude that Bitcoin is backed by the computational resources used for mining, this is insufficient to explain how it acquires its value. Here is a brief overview of economics necessary to comprehend it.

When fiat currency was first introduced, it was backed by gold. Since people believed in gold, they also believed in currency. After a long period, the currency became fully dependent on governments and no longer backed by gold. Nevertheless, individuals continued to believe in it because they created or contributed to the creation of their democracy. Since governments guarantee its value and the public trusts it, it achieves that value. In an international context, the value of a country's currency is determined by various variables, the most critical of which is 'supply and demand.' Bear in mind that some countries that printed an excessive amount of fiat currency notes went bankrupt; their economies suffered! There must be a balance, and understanding this requires different economics, which is beyond the reach of this book. Therefore, let us return to Bitcoin for the time being.

However, before we talk about the fluctuation in Bitcoin's price against U.S. dollars, let us get acquainted with the basic supply and demand concept. Did you know that a product's price fluctuates mainly due to a change in supply and demand? In the first scenario, we will look at price fluctuation due to the change in demand.

Suppose Clara lives in Geneva, Switzerland. The prices of eco-friendly products in Geneva, such as solar lamps and rechargeable batteries, are stable for the given moment. Suddenly, several environment protection campaigns take place inside Switzerland, after which the Swiss government bans the use of all environmentally harmful products. Now the Swiss economy witnesses a major inclination of the public towards eco-friendly products. As the demand for environmentally friendly items grows, so does the cost of those products. When Clara compares the old and new prices of solar lamps in Geneva, she notices a 13% increase. Hence, the increased demand pushes the prices upwards.

In the second scenario, we will see how a change in the supply of a product can shift its prices up or down. Imagine you are a sportsperson. Your favorite brand's sports kit is part of your regular workout. One day you hear the news of the labor shortage in the sports industry. Due to a labor shortage, your favorite sports brand must cut its supply of sports products, but the demand remains the same. Since the sports products cannot meet the demand, there will be a shortage of sports goods from the given brand. This shortage in the supply of sports products will push their prices up.

A similar supply and demand mechanism applies to Bitcoin. I will give you my example with regards to the supply and demand forces of Bitcoin. During the years when I was trading in stocks, I would frequently hear about Bitcoin. However, since the concept of cryptocurrency was new then, traders or consumers, for that matter, had little awareness about this form of digital currency. Therefore, when Bitcoin was first released, it lacked an official price or value to place their confidence. If anyone were to sell it for some U.S. dollars (USD), I would never have purchased them in the first place. When the exchange began, it gradually established a price, and one Bitcoin was not even worth 1 USD at the time. Bitcoin is a scarce resource because Bitcoin is mined through a competitive and decentralized method called 'mining.' They are generated at a fixed rate with a maximum limit of 21 million Bitcoin ever created. Now, reverting to the game of 'supply and demand,' the value of Bitcoin began to inflate. Slowly, as the whole world came to believe in it, its price skyrocketed from a few USD to thousands of USD. Bitcoin adoption is increasing at a rate never seen before among consumers, retailers, start-ups, and large businesses since they are used as currency. Thus, the value of Bitcoin is strongly affected by 'confidence,' 'adoption,' and 'supply and demand,' with the market setting the price.

The question now is why Bitcoin's value is so volatile at the time of writing and fluctuates so much. A straightforward explanation is 'supply and demand.' We have discovered that there can be only a finite number of Bitcoin in circulation, 21 million and that the rate at which they have been produced decreases over time. Because of this, there is always a supply-demand imbalance, resulting in this volatility.

Additionally, Bitcoins are never exchanged in a single location. There are several exchanges located worldwide, and each exchange has its own set of exchange rates. The indexes you see in a trading platform collect and average bitcoin trading rates from several exchanges. Again, since none of these indexes obtain data from the same set of exchanges, they do not correspond.

Some of the leading Bitcoin exchanges in 2021 include:

- Coinbase
- Binance
- Bitcoin IRA
- Prime XBT

Similarly, the liquidity factor, which refers to the total number of Bitcoin flowing through the market at any given moment, impacts the price volatility of Bitcoin. At the moment, it is unquestionably a high-risk asset, but it may stabilize over time. For example, consider the following factors that can affect the supply and demand for Bitcoin, and therefore their price:

- The public's trust in Bitcoin and their fear of uncertainty

- Press coverage on both positive and negative Bitcoin news

- Some people hold Bitcoin and do not circulate throughout the market, whereas others constantly buy and sell to reduce danger. Therefore, Bitcoin's liquidity ratio fluctuates.

- Acceptance of Bitcoin by the world's largest e-commerce companies

- Particular countries' prohibition of Bitcoin

If you are wondering whether Bitcoin can crash, then certainly, the answer is 'Yes.' Numerous countries' currency systems have collapsed in many instances. To be sure, there were political and economic causes for them to crash, such as hyperinflation, which is not the case with Bitcoin, which cannot be produced indefinitely, and the total number of Bitcoin is set. However, Bitcoin can fail due to technological or cryptographic issues.

Let us have an example from recent history. Bitcoin's price recently sank by nearly 30% after the Chinese regulators' announcement to ban payment firms and banks from utilizing cryptocurrencies. However, the real selloff started after Elon Musk, Tesla's founder, revealed his failure to accept Bitcoin against car purchases. Interestingly, Bitcoin once again surged by more than 12% in value after the Tesla owner hinted about developing the Dogecoin.

Keeping all our facts and figures straight, it is important to note that Bitcoin has withstood the test of time ever since its inception in 2008, and there is a chance that it will continue to grow significantly larger over time, but this cannot be guaranteed!

But whatever the case may be, an interesting fact about Bitcoin is that it cannot be banned from circulating. Some countries, including Bolivia, Thailand, Vietnam, and Bangladesh, tried to restrict bitcoin usage. However, other countries such as Russia, Japan, Australia, and Venezuela use Bitcoin just as a fiat currency.

Bitcoin's future appears to be both certain and unstoppable. Nobody knows for certain what will happen, but it seems that Bitcoin has penetrated deep enough into the mainstream that it cannot be reversed. Numerous major industries, including airlines, technology firms, government agencies, and the financial sector, have begun to embrace Bitcoin and, even more importantly, the underlying blockchain technology. The growing demand for skilled blockchain programmers across various industries demonstrates that the blockchain age has arrived.

A new generation of entrepreneurs has emerged in the cryptocurrency and blockchain space, creating novel applications based on Bitcoin as a currency and a technology. Only time can say if Bitcoin as a currency will continue to appreciate and continue to rule the cryptocurrency markets or if a disruptive newcomer will dethrone it. Diversifying your cryptocurrency holdings is seen to improve your chances of choosing a winner.

Cryptocurrency diversification is a routine that I have been practicing for a long time now. I can explain the diversification by endorsing the expression: 'don't put all your eggs in one basket.' Logic says that if you accidentally drop the basket, no more eggs will be left. The same goes for cryptocurrencies. Crypto diversification means investing in multiple crypto projects instead of placing everything in one or two projects. Right now, I have invested in the following different types of cryptocurrencies:

- Bitcoin (BTC)

- Ethereum (ETH)

- Tezos (XTZ)

- Iota (MIOTA)

- Radix (eXRD)

- Namecoin (NMC)

What do I get from diversifying my crypto portfolio? Following are some benefits I get:

- I protect against risks.

- I gain more knowledge on different crypto projects and coins.

- I have more opportunities to achieve better performance.

Therefore, the crux is that although my priority is Bitcoin, it is prudent to invest in others.

Hearing tales of early Bitcoin adopters who made millions can make newcomers to Bitcoin feel as if they are too late. Though it is unknown if Bitcoin would be the 'one coin to rule them all,' the promise of blockchain technology is only now starting to gain traction in the mainstream, bubbling to the surface of a vast sea of opportunity. Of course, no crystal ball will reveal the exact shape of the future, but one thing is certain: this is just the beginning. Five or ten years from now, individuals who make prudent investments today might very well be considered 'early adopters.'

Understanding the Bitcoin Mechanism

Patricia just completed her graduation. Alongside her studies, she had been learning about the Bitcoin investment. She is extremely excited to get started with Bitcoin. Patricia knows that to get started, she needs a good internet connection and a smartphone to download the Bitcoin wallet. Although these wallets come in four different forms, mobile, desktop, hardware, and web, she chose the mobile wallet. According to Patricia, she can store her Bitcoin in her mobile wallet, a software program. However, technically, she knows the Bitcoin is not stored anywhere. Once Patricia has a balance in her Bitcoin wallet, she will get a secret number called a private key. The private key will represent the Bitcoin address of her wallet. Patricia says that her bitcoin wallet will let her send or receive the Bitcoin under her ownership.

Did you see how easily Patricia got started with her Bitcoin? To get started with Bitcoin, no technical knowledge is needed. All you need to do is to download a Bitcoin wallet and get started. When you download and install a wallet on your laptop or mobile device, the wallet automatically creates your first Bitcoin address (public key). You will, and should, produce several more. If you want to maintain anonymity, then it is recommended that you only use the Bitcoin addresses once. Though it works, address reuse is an unintentional consequence of Bitcoin. Reusing addresses can jeopardize privacy and confidentiality. For instance, if you reuse an address and sign a transaction with the same private key, the receiver can easily and accurately verify that the address is yours. If the same address is used for multiple transactions, they can all be monitored, making it much easier to determine who you are. Bear in mind that Bitcoin is not fully anonymous. It is referred to as pseudonymous, and there are methods for tracing the source of transactions that can expose the owners.

You must provide the person transferring Bitcoin to you with your Bitcoin address. This is extremely safe, as the public key is already public. We know that Bitcoin has no concept of a closing balance and that all transactions are registered. Bitcoin wallets can easily measure their spendable balances since they have the private keys to the public keys used to receive transactions. Numerous wallet providers offer a range of Bitcoin wallets. There are numerous types of wallets, each with a different level of security: mobile wallets, desktop wallets, browser-based online wallets, and hardware wallets. When working with Bitcoin, you must exercise extreme caution about wallet protection. Payments made with Bitcoin are final.

You are probably wondering how stable these wallets are. To be honest, various wallet types provide varying degrees of protection, and it all depends on how you plan to use it. Numerous online wallet services have been compromised. Enabling two-factor authentication wherever possible is often a good idea. If you are a frequent Bitcoin consumer, it might be prudent to hold small amounts in your wallets and the remainder in a secure location. An offline wallet, also known as a cold wallet, is not linked to the Internet and thus offers the highest degree of protection for savings. Additionally, there should be adequate backup plans in place for your wallet if you lose your computer/mobile device. Bear in mind that if you lose your private key, you will also lose all related funds.

If you have not entered Bitcoin as a miner running a full node, you could simply be a Bitcoin user or trader. You will undoubtedly need an exchange from which you can purchase Bitcoin using U.S. dollars or other currencies that the exchanges recognize. You should always choose to purchase Bitcoin from a reputable and stable exchange. Numerous examples exist of exchanges that security breaches have compromised.

Security

To help envision the cryptocurrency and Blockchain more clearly, consider Fort Knox. Fort Knox is famous for housing the United States' gold bullion depository. Fort Knox contains a boatload of gold. Fort Knox safeguards this gold with armed guards, blast-proof vaults, and several other onsite security measures. If gold has to be transported, we can envision armored vehicles and soldiers armed with machine guns keeping an eye on the process. It would be incredibly difficult for a thief to break into Fort Knox and steal the gold, not just because of the fortified compound but also because gold is a heavy physical object that would be difficult to transport.

Banks (and many other institutions) have traditionally followed a similar model for asset protection, centralizing everything and relying on layers of security. However, the vast majority of financial information is now stored digitally as data. Of course, we trust banks to provide the cash necessary to back up the numbers in our bank accounts, but for the vast majority of people, those numbers represent a record of value rather than a physical cash sum stashed in a safe.

Rather than physical vaults, our financial assets are mainly represented by financial data stored in the server of the bank's 'digital vault.' Banks aim to turn these servers into digital Fort Knox, but this centralized paradigm does not translate well to the new world of digital transactions. Whereas breaking into Fort Knox and stealing gold will require a large amount of dynamite, special equipment, escape vehicles, and Ocean's 11-style finesse, hackers can break into bank servers and steal financial information on a fairly regular basis using only computers. As a result, credit card fraud, identity theft, and data breaches are all serious risks that financial institutions face on a near-daily basis.

Banks continue to add layers of protection to their 'digital vaults,' though hackers continue to breach them. Fort Knox works well for storing physical tons of gold, but it fails miserably when applied to digital data. Let's look at the matter from a different perspective. We can begin to wonder if, rather than secure one central server, there is a better model for storing digital information and processing digital transactions. This is where blockchain technology comes into play.

Each block in the Blockchain is connected to the previous block and is publicly recorded through many different nodes located throughout the world. Therefore, rather than hacking into a single central server and stealing or manipulating data, a hacker will have to modify the entire Blockchain simultaneously through most computers that store it worldwide.

Technically, this would take an enormous amount of computational capacity, rendering it effectively impossible to do under current conditions. The blockchain system is designed to be stable due to the lack of centralized data storage. If anyone attempts to enter a false transaction, such as giving themselves Bitcoin that does not exist, the numerous computers that manage the Blockchain will notice that the math does not add up. If the math does not add up, the transaction is considered invalid and denied and is not added to the blockchain record.

Chapter 2. Why Make Trading in Crypto and How to Earn in Crypto?

T here are a couple of ways you can make money with cryptocurrencies, including mining, trading, and ICO (Initial Coin Offering). But, to get started with cryptocurrencies, you need to first buy some. And you buy it by exchanging your national currencies or any other cryptocurrencies (e.g., Ethereum) by using an exchange. Now that you have some cryptocurrencies, here are some of the best ways to make money with cryptocurrencies:

- **Mining:** Mining can be tricky, especially for newbies. However, if you are extremely tech-savvy and have a lot of time to invest in learning the ropes, then it is definitely an option.

- **Trading:** This is a simple technique to earn money that you can perform from your smartphone or a computer. However, trading requires you to study the markets and patterns, so it can be a time-consuming process.

- **Initial Coin Offering**: ICOs have become very popular in recent times and have provided a lot of people with a lot of money. However, this is also an option that is quite risky and a lot of people have lost money as a result.

- **Staking:** Staking involves holding on to your coins for a longer period and getting rewarded for doing so.

- **Masternodes:** These are very similar to staking, and you can easily run one using a VPS or a dedicated server.

- **Trading bots:** While trading bots can be a good way to make money, they are not without risks and you will be trading with bots and not humans.

- **Tip bots:** This is an easy and simple way to earn some instant money. You just need to follow a few rules and you will be rewarded for doing so.

- **Gambling:** You can easily gamble on the numerous casinos that are available.

- **Faucets:** These are simple ways to make money. However, you need to invest a lot of time to get a payout.

- **Folding:** You can also make money by folding proteins.

- **Mining rig rental:** You can rent out your rig and make some good money by doing so.

- **Cloud mining:** Cloud mining is also a great way to make money. It involves buying mining power from someone else in an easier, simpler manner.

- **Bitcoin flipping:** Bitcoin flipping is yet another way to make money. You will buy bitcoins at a low price and sell them when the price is high.

- **Trading options:** You can also trade options, although you need to have a good knowledge of trading options.

- **Trading forex:** You can also trade forex with cryptocurrencies.

Trading Cryptocurrencies: How to Start

To begin trading with cryptocurrencies, you must first obtain them. You can obtain them either by purchasing them or by mining them.

- **Buy cryptocurrencies:** You can easily buy cryptocurrencies with your credit card on Unocoin.

You can also buy them with your debit card or net banking. But the problem is that you can only buy one or two cryptocurrencies using your debit or credit card. You can also buy them on Koinex. However, you can only buy a few cryptocurrencies with your credit card.

- **Trading cryptocurrencies:** You can also trade with cryptocurrencies on Koinex and Zebpay. You can also trade with cryptocurrencies on Bitfinex, a popular trading platform.

- **Mining:** You can easily mine some cryptocurrencies like Ethereum and Zcash with cloud mining. A lot of people have made a lot of money by mining cryptocurrencies and you can too by following the right steps.

- **Earn free cryptocurrencies:** You can also earn free cryptocurrencies by taking part in airdrops and bounties. I have already taken part in a few airdrops and have earned quite a lot of free cryptocurrencies.

- **Earn with cryptocurrencies:** There are a lot of ways you can earn with cryptocurrencies. I have already mentioned a couple of them above.

- **Exchange cryptocurrencies**: You can also exchange your cryptocurrencies for any other cryptocurrencies or national currencies. You can easily do this by using an exchange platform.

- **Staking:** You can also earn by staking your coins for a longer time.

- **Masternodes:** You can also earn by running a Masternode with a VPS or a dedicated server.

- **Trading bots:** You can also earn money by investing in trading bots.

- **Tip bots:** You can also earn by following certain rules given by a tip bot.

- **Trading signals:** You can make money with trading signals by paying a certain fee to a trading signal provider.

- **Faucets:** You can earn money by faucets. However, in order to get paid for a faucet, you need to invest a lot of time.

- **Mining rig rental:** You can earn money by renting out your rig. However, you need to have a good rig in order to be able to earn money with mining rig rental.

- **Cloud mining:** You can also earn money by mining on cloud mining platforms. A few of the popular cloud mining platforms are IcloudMining and HashFlare.

- **Bitcoin flipping:** You can also earn money by flipping bitcoins.

- **Trading options:** You can also earn money by trading options. You can easily start trading with cryptocurrencies by using some trading options. For example, you can start trading with Bitcoin using a trading platform like Poloniex.

Buy and Sell Cryptos

Once you have some cryptocurrencies, you can decide to buy more using services like Coinbase, Binance, or Bittrex (although these are not the only ones). However, if you are not comfortable buying cryptocurrencies on these exchanges, then you can always use these services for buying cryptocurrencies with a bank account.

Once you have your cryptocurrencies, you can exchange them for other altcoins, including altcoins that have recently started to gain popularity such as Ripple, Cardano, and Stellar, among others.

You can also buy and sell cryptos, which is quite easy to do. However, the process of buying and selling cryptos can be lengthy and can take a lot of time. This is because you need to study the markets and patterns.

However, if you want to make some good money, then you can buy bitcoins and sell them when they are relatively cheap. You can put your bitcoins to a variety of uses now that you have them.

Even if you are not interested in buying and selling cryptos, you can always keep a few as a form of savings, especially if you have a lot of them.

What Is the Best Way to Earn Money With Cryptocurrencies?

Many people are not interested in making money with cryptocurrencies, but if you want to earn some extra money, then the best way to do so is by using a cryptocurrency exchange. But, before you choose the best exchange to use, there are a few things you need to consider:

- **Ease of use:** This is a major factor to consider, especially if you are new to this. Do not be too concerned about the interface for most exchanges as most of them have a very good user interface.

- **Fiat vs crypto trading:** You need to make sure that the exchange you are choosing allows you to trade in both crypto and fiat currencies.

- **Low fees:** You should not choose an exchange that has extremely high fees. The fees should be relatively lower and you should also know how you will make money from the exchange.

- **Customer support:** Customer support is also a major factor to consider. Many exchanges have excellent customer support and you can easily reach out to them via phone and live chat.

- **Security:** You should also make sure that the exchange you are using is secure and does not have any security issues that could put your funds at risk.

- **SEO:** You should also consider SEO, especially if you are using an exchange that is not as popular. If you are using a popular exchange, then you will not have much of a need to do SEO.

- **Low trading volume:** Low trading volume indicates that the exchange is not centralized and that they are easier to hack. You should also pick an exchange with a small trading volume.

- **Localized and supported currencies:** You should also look to see that the exchange you are using supports local currencies and is not restricted to depositing and withdrawing in only a few cryptocurrencies.

- **Ease of funding:** If you are using an exchange that gives you the option to fund it using a bank account, then you can have access to a lot of options to make money with cryptocurrencies.

- **Customer support and customer service:** You should also look for an exchange that has excellent customer support and customer service. You can easily reach them by phone or email.

- **OTC Arbitrage:** This is another way you can make money with cryptocurrencies. This involves you looking for an opportunity in volatile markets, such as the crypto markets, and buying cryptocurrency when you see an opportunity.

Chapter 3. What Is NFT and How to Earn With NFT

What is an NFT?

An NFT (non-fungible token) is a crypto token that is unique and has a value. The obvious token within the blockchain industry is bitcoin, so it would stand to reason that an NFT could be used to go against the blockchain.

However, bitcoin has become too popular in the market nowadays; if we were to create another currency that was very similar to bitcoin except with added features of its own, we could create an NFT blockchain. This could be part of a completely new cryptocurrency or it can be decided by any company within the blockchain industry to set up their own token-based ecosystem.

For example, a fungible token could be something like Monero, where one 'token' of Monero is the same as any other 'token.' However, if you took an NFT and broke it down into smaller pieces like dice, each piece would still have the same value as others. This is because each token would preserve its value and be similar to the others no matter how many times it was broken down, cut up, or rearranged. Each piece of the block is its own token with its own value.

Now, if you could create a token within the blockchain that has the same characteristics as Monero and Bitcoin then it would be an NFT.

How to Earn With NFT?

There are ways in which we can earn with NFTs. First of all, a company within the blockchain industry can decide that they want to create their own NFT cryptocurrency ecosystem. For example, if one wanted to set up their own decentralized app (dApp) then there is no reason why they couldn't create their own token for use in this dApp ecosystem.

The second way is that a company within the blockchain industry could create its own token for use within the dApp ecosystem. For example, if you wanted to build a decentralized version of Netflix then you could create a token to be used in this ecosystem. Alternatively, you could also set up your own tokens and let people earn by using these tokens in your dApp. The tokens can be used within your ecosystem as a means of exchange between users.

This is where it begins to get interesting because there is no reason why companies can't use NFTs to create their own ecosystems within the blockchain and have people earn by using these tokens within this ecosystem.

The third way is to engage in the exchange of NFTs into a particular currency like Bitcoin, Ether, or another cryptocurrency. For example, you could create an NFT token to be used within your decentralized marketplace and your users could earn with tokens by using those tokens in your system. You would then be engaging in the trading of your own NFT token onto another blockchain; this could mean that users will be able to earn with this new type of cryptocurrency by using it within your marketplace ecosystem.

The last method is for people to create their own NFT token for use within their dApp or marketplace. This could be done through different blockchain platforms like Ethereum and NEO. It could also be done using other platforms like Komodo or even through the use of POW systems like Bitcoin. So, if you wanted to start a new NFT on one of these platforms, you could purchase into the platform and start earning with it.

Final Thoughts

This is just a purely speculative idea and at this stage, it is highly unlikely that this will ever become a reality. However, if we were ever to do away with Bitcoin altogether then an NFT blockchain could help to push the blockchain industry forward again. It would make sense for an individual company within the blockchain industry to create its own token-based ecosystem because it would make more sense than creating one based on bitcoin.

So, if a company within the blockchain industry wanted to create a new NFT blockchain they could do this by creating their own token and engaging in the trading of that token onto another blockchain. This could be done within a decentralized marketplace or dApp ecosystem and this could be achieved through different blockchains such as Ethereum and NEO.

This idea is massively speculative but if we were to ever go back to creating our own tokens on blockchains instead of bitcoin for traditional fiat then it would make sense. Of course, some type of regulation is required to ensure that malevolent actors are unable to commit crimes using these tokens, but adding regulation will significantly slow down the process.

There is no reason why companies can't build their own token ecosystems and let their users earn with those tokens by using them in those app ecosystems. It's an idea that makes sense if we ever wanted to go back to the old way but with added features of blockchain technology.

This is why it would make sense for an individual company within the blockchain industry to create their own tokens; they could do this on different platforms such as Ethereum, NEO, Komodo, and even POW systems like Bitcoin. This is because they already have these technical pre-requisites set up which could help them to create their own NFT ecosystem.

Chapter 4. What Is NFT Art and How Can It Help You Make Money?

NFT stands for 'non-fungible token' or 'non-fungible right.' It refers to a new type of digital asset that cannot be duplicated within a certain set limit. NFTs are made of a variety of asset classes, such as rights, goods, and artwork. As blockchain technology has become more accessible in recent years, many creators have been using it to create new types of tokens that represent different forms of value. Traditionally these tokens have been analyzed on the ERC-721 protocol on the Ethereum blockchain. In contrast, NFT Art is a term that refers to artworks made on the ERC-721 protocol.

The addition of NFT Art to the ecosystem will help provide a practical application for blockchain technology and utilize the value that has existed in creative work. NFT Art aims to redefine the blockchain industry by increasing the value of creative works themselves through decentralized implementation. The sense of value derived from creative work is established via many factors including its price, fame, ownership, and rarity. While artists may produce multiple copies of their work, each copy earns less value than the original version. This leads to limitations when valuing works based strictly on their ownership or selling price.

Asset valuation is a means to measure the value of an account through the assets it holds. Similar to traditional investments, there are also digital art investment vehicles such as auction trading platforms and art galleries. Investment in artworks is typically concentrated in the established artworks of renowned artists. This limits investment opportunities for new artists whose works do not yet have much credibility in value because they are either untested or have no record of sales.

With blockchain technology, we can use a public asset accounting ledger to record transactions and make a unique ID for each artwork along with concrete ownership records. This allows us to clearly identify ownership and provide a standard valuation for each piece of artwork that can be easily accessed by buyers on the market for investment or purchase purposes. NFT art transactions are recorded and stored within the ledger of an NFT Art blockchain.

This solution to establish the value of artwork provides a new way to view existing assets and enables artists to build their own collection of artworks that they can use as investment vehicles or a way to form their own private collection. This will encourage artists, investors, collectors, and art enthusiasts alike to benefit from the implementation of NFT Art into the market.

How Do You Earn With NFT Art?

The process for earning with a piece of NFT art is similar in concept to how one would collect dividends from an asset or participate in a traditional stock market index fund. The following steps are performed in the process of buying and holding a piece of NFT art:

1. Purchase the asset from an artist or an auction trading platform. The owner of the art can also choose to raffle or auction off their artwork to investors and collectors on an open exchange like OpenSea.

2. Wait for the asset to appreciate over time. This will occur as the art appreciates in value and its popularity increases. An increase in demand for a piece of NFT art will lead to increased price volatility. This volatility is especially prominent when a particular NFT artwork is featured online, on traditional media

outlets, or used by public figures like celebrities, influencers, athletes, or politicians. The value of an NFT piece will increase as it gains publicity.

3. Convert the asset into a fungible token by transferring ownership of the art to a registered NFT Art wallet on an exchange or decentralized application (dApp). This can be achieved through the transfer to a user's personal Bitcoin or Ethereum wallet, or a compatible NFT Art wallet such as Etherisc.

4. Receive dividends from the asset. The artist of the artwork is credited with 3% of the profit derived from each transaction that occurs when that specific artwork is sold. The earnings distributed to artists will be paid out in Ether (ETH) and are paid out weekly on average.

5. Convert the fungible token back into the asset. If the asset is ever converted to another type of fungible token, payment in Ether is required. There are currently only a few decentralized exchanges that allow users to exchange and trade NFTs with one another. Since NFT Art is a relatively new concept in the cryptocurrency and technology industry, many users have had difficulty exchanging their NFT

tokens for traditional fiat currency (USD) or other cryptocurrencies.

The first implementation of an ERC-721 as an alternative NFT token was created by Tezos with its XTZ token. This implementation of an ERC-721 token has been distributed to all users who have verified their accounts on the Tezos blockchain.

The XTZ token was created without an initial supply limit and is distributed to users at a rate of 0.1% each year. The distribution will continue until 100% of the tokens have been distributed among users with a verified account. These tokens can be held by any user who owns them and the XTZ token has no designated method for how it will be used or traded on the Tezos network, unlike other cryptocurrencies and ERC-20 tokens that specify how tokens are used for specific purposes on their respective blockchain networks.

The first NFT Art token, named Ether-Powered NFT Art Tokens (EPNAA) will be compatible with the Ethereum network and provides three main benefits to the value of each piece of artwork. An initial supply cap of 100 million tokens will be generated for the EPNAA token. This initial supply cap combined with an inflation rate of around 10% per year. Over time, each piece of artwork is expected to appreciate in value through usage on different media outlets and social media platforms. The EPNAA token will also act as a reward for users who own NFT art tokens, so it serves as a more practical application than other types of cryptocurrencies and ERC-20 tokens due to its usage on the Ethereum blockchain itself.

How to Create an NFT Art Blockchain?

A company or individual may want to create their own NFT Art blockchain to better maintain records of ownership, usage, and trading of artwork. If a person or company wishes to start their own NFT Art blockchain, they can sign up for a trial on the OpenSea network. From here, they can then create their own NFT Art asset and set up their own private marketplace for users and artists. Fees for using this service range from 0.5% to 2% depending on which features are included in the initial development of the platform.

These blockchain-based platforms allow users to create NFT Art tokens and keep them private or publicly available. Once deployed to the public blockchain, these tokens can be transferred between users with a compatible NFT Art wallet. This creates a system where each piece of artwork is assigned a unique identifier and can be traced back to its original owner or artist. Transitioning from an ERC-20 token on the Ethereum network to an ERC-721 token on the Ethereum network through smart contract would be simple because the Ethereum network has already been introduced as one of the most popular blockchains for managing transactions for cryptocurrencies like Bitcoin (smart contracts are computer programs that facilitate, verify, or enforce the negotiation or performance of a contract).

There are several benefits to using the Ethereum network for NFT Art blockchain development. Since the Ethereum network is so popular, the developer can expect a large number of users to purchase and use their tokenized artwork along with their decentralized marketplace. This will lead to a larger user base and greater adoption of the platform. By creating an ERC-721 token on an existing platform, developers can also make sure that they have access to open-source code from other NFT Art dApps and support from other cryptocurrency enthusiasts.

Chapter 5. What Is DeFi and How to Earn With DeFi?

DeFi is a decentralized and blockchain-based platform that creates peer-to-peer online courses, where software developers and learners get paid. Taught by top Ethereum experts and live in a virtual classroom setting, these courses provide you with the expertise needed to develop your skillset in one of the most popular programming languages.

The many ways you can earn with DeFi include: paying for courses through cryptocurrency, in exchange for your skills—giving back what is learned to improve future course design, or giving back to the community. This section will hopefully help show you how easy it is to learn something new from an expert with DeFi.

DeFi is a new type of online course platform, based on Ethereum smart contracts and the Interplanetary File System (IPFS). It is completely decentralized, which means there is no central authority. Anyone can create a course on DeFi with no need for approval. We believe it to be the first online education platform that allows you to earn cryptocurrency by giving back to the community or paying your course fees with cryptocurrency.

The decentralized aspect is achieved through blockchain technology. The process of creating a course is similar to how we create and manage files on our cloud storage portals such as Dropbox or Google Drive. The DeFi uses an Interplanetary File System (IPFS) where you can build and share files called courses between people via a decentralized peer-to-peer network. This allows for the creation of secure multiplayer courses, in which you can learn from multiple sources at once, without the need for a central control point those controls what you are allowed to see and when.

By using an IPFS, every time a course is updated on DeFi, everyone who is a part of the course will download the latest version. The updating system works by adding data to new blocks that are part of the blockchain.

How Does DeFi Work?

DeFi uses a tokenized system, which means that there is no central authority for managing and updating courses. Instead, everything on DeFi runs through smart contracts based on Ethereum. The system is designed to be open with no limits on what can be built in terms of educational content. This means that anyone can create a course and teach anything. The only thing that is required is knowledge.

The tokenized system allows for students to pay for courses with DeFi tokens, while they are also rewarded with DeFi tokens if they provide inputs that are valuable to future course updates. By using DeFi tokens, you encourage the community to reward those members who provide valuable inputs, which makes it an education platform that rewards helpful learners rather than commercializing courses.

Chapter 6. Trade in Crypto

With the advent of cryptocurrencies, money (or crypto) transactions are now easier than ever to conduct. Nonetheless, there are steps that you need to take in order to properly trade in crypto. It's never too late to educate yourself, which is why we've laid out how it all goes down. Listen up and learn more about trading in crypto now!

Find the Right Platform

There are plenty of platforms available where you can trade cryptocurrency for cash or other cryptocurrencies. You can compare their features so that you can decide which to use for your needs. Some platforms allow for recurring deposits and withdrawals, while others require instant or one-time deposits. On some platforms, you may also purchase and trade cryptocurrencies with a credit or debit card.

Trading platforms usually have their own set of fees, which they pass on to their users. They may also charge other fees such as the listing fee, transaction fees, and withdrawal fees.

Before settling on a platform, review the fees so that you are aware of their policy.

Also, think of your time spent trading in crypto as an investment as well and make sure you're spending enough time with it. Having dedicated trading time is a must if you want to do well in your trading project.

Get Some Tips on the Trade

It's crucial to consider the details involved in the process and how they may be handled easily before you start trading in cryptocurrency. The trade itself is easy, but you should make sure to master the steps involved so that you can handle all of them well.

Your first step is to choose a cryptocurrency that you want to trade and then invest in it. You should think of what coin would suit your purpose best because of its market cap, supply cap, and price. Then, do some research on the coin so that you know all about it. You must know if there are any ICOs happening soon for this currency and how much money will be raised from them.

This is the first step that you have to take when trading in crypto. Try to find a coin that you want to invest in and then research it.

Find the Right Platform

Once you've decided on a coin, it's important to find the right platform that will allow you to trade in it. For instance, there are platforms such as Binance and Coinbase where you can trade your favorite cryptocurrency of choice. Some platforms accept all major cryptocurrencies like Poloniex and Bittrex, which accept almost all coins out there. These platforms allow you to trade from your computer or mobile phone.

Select Your Coin

After you have found the right trading platform and are able to register an account there, it's time to think about the coin that you want in order to buy it. There are plenty of coins out there, but not all of them are worth investing in or trading in. Before you choose the right coin, compare it to the rest of them and make sure it's one of the best out there. Don't get swayed by its price alone because not all coins are worth investing in.

You should also check their market cap and supply cap so that you can distinguish between a good and bad coin. Generally, coins with a high market cap (a lot of units in circulation) are more valuable than those with a lower market cap or supply cap. There is no set formula to determine this value ratio except through calculation.

To help you find the best coin, look at how popular it is among other traders and how well it is performing on different exchanges. A coin with a high trading volume is usually worth investing in as it means more people are looking to trade in it. The higher the trading volume, the better for you.

You're never wrong when you choose a coin that has performed well in the past and has a loyal community of users behind it. These are always your best bet when it comes to finding that perfect coin with which to trade in crypto.

Choose Your Base Currency

Before you make any trades, it's important to select one base currency that you will use for all of them. For instance, if you want to make an Ethereum trade, you should use ETH as your base currency. Your base currency will be the main currency in which you'll be conducting your trades, so you must choose wisely.

You can also have more than one base currency for trading in crypto if you wish so. However, this is only recommended for experienced traders who know what they're doing.

Make Some Trades

You've reached the last step before deciding on your strategy for trading in crypto! From here, you can choose to begin trading or wait and watch how the market moves first to get a better idea of its behavior.

Think of Your Strategy

Once you have several coins trading in crypto, or even just one or two, it's time to think of your own strategy for trading in crypto. Remember that it's important to have a definite and clear strategy so that you can improve your overall results. To be able to do this, you should consider all factors involved with the market and trade accordingly.

The main factors you should consider are:

- **Your base currency.** What is the base currency you are using to trade in crypto? What is the value of it? These factors will determine the limits and potentials of your trades.

- **Your trading times.** You must decide on a trading time or an algorithm that you can use to make trades in your chosen coin at regular intervals. If a coin is performing well, plan on making your next trade after two weeks minimum and six months maximum. If a coin has started performing poorly, plan on making your next trade after 24 hours or six months maximum depending on how quickly it recovers.

- **The market conditions of any given day or week that you plan to trade in crypto.** You must be familiar with market conditions before you can make any trades.

- **Your trading volumes.** What is the volume of your base currency or the total value that you want to trade? This is necessary in order to calculate how many coins you'll receive and their worth. When calculating your trading volume, all figures should be based on your base currency's value.

- **Your profits.** How much profit do you want from every trade? You have to set a profit target for each coin as well as for each transaction. Your goal with this should be to not just make money but to also increase your trading capital.

There are also other factors that you can consider such as market psychology, but these are things experts only have to think about. It's best if you just stick to the basic factors and make them work for you.

Make Your First Trade

Now that you've planned your trading strategy, it's time to put it into action. Instead of swapping all of your coins minute by minute or second by second, you can store part of them in your account for safekeeping. This is when 'hodling' comes in handy, which is the act of holding on to your cryptocurrency instead of selling it quickly.

However, if you have a strategy in place and some money in your account, you can trade with them right away or at predetermined periods. You can also decide whether or not to trade with other people's coins or their HODLing tips. This is something that only seasoned traders should consider as it's a bad practice for beginners and will only cause them to lose out on profits.

Take Profits When the Time Is Right

When you are ready to take profits from your trades, you should do it as soon as possible so as not to lose out on any of the benefits that come with it. The longer you wait, the more chance you have of losing out on profits you could have gained from the start.

A good way to make a profit is to do it gradually once your target has been reached. This allows you to keep a portion of your profits safely in your account while still allowing you to use the rest of it for future trades.

You can also choose to use such strategies as averaging down or cutting losses and taking them as a whole. By doing so, your losses will be minimized and your gains maximized, which is what trading in crypto is all about. The best thing about this is that no matter which strategy you choose, it's good to use both at the same time, one to minimize losses and the other to maximize gains. This way, you won't end up with just a few winners but with a lot of them instead.

Take Losses When They Come Your Way

While taking profits as soon as they come your way is something you should be doing, it's also important that you learn how to take losses when they come your way instead of trying to wait and hope for profits in the future. This will not only help you save your overall profits for future trades that may come your way shortly but will also teach you how to work with a possible loss.

When you can actually live with your losses, it's easier to take them when they come your way and then move on from them so that you can continue making other trades.

Using Available Resources and Information

Apart from the guide that we've provided here, there are also a lot of resources out there on the internet about trading in crypto. There are videos, tutorials, and even books that you can read about the subject if necessary.

To get the most out of these resources, you should familiarize yourself with some of the terms used in the cryptocurrency and trading world. This will allow you to learn faster and understand better what's being said. It will also allow you to produce more profits from your trading with less effort.

Chapter 7. Identifying Top Performing

We went through the reasons why cryptocurrency investment or trading is the way forward. It is certainly more rewarding than stock markets, and it can certainly provide everyone with ample chances to gain more for their investments. Whether you are a first-time investor or a seasoned one, investing in cryptocurrencies can only become rewarding if you know the cryptocurrencies to focus on.

This is what would generally happen if you are a first-time investor.

You awoke one fine morning and concluded, 'Well, today is the day I invest in cryptos.' All excited, you decided to invest $1,000 to see how it goes. You go to google and search for 'Where to buy cryptocurrencies' and find yourself bombarded by so many marketplaces offering 'the best rates.'

Let's assume that you decided to stick with Binance as it offers direct credit card purchases and also allows you to transfer cryptocurrencies you already have from your wallet.

You rush through and click on 'Market,' and that's pretty much where things leave you speechless.

'Holy… There are so many!'

That's exactly the problem people face immediately when they first decide to venture into cryptocurrency investing. Simply put, there are far too many choices to consider. One is literally lost trying to figure out which are the ones they should go for. As of January 20, 2021, there were a total of 7,812 crypto assets to choose from (Wanguba, n.d.). That's a significant number, especially considering that most of us only know about Bitcoin and Ethereum. And to be more accurate, Ethereum is not even a cryptocurrency. It is the blockchain on which the cryptocurrency Ether is on. Somehow people get confused between Ether and Ethereum.

Think about it. What are the first three names that pop up whenever someone mentions the word 'cryptos?' Let me spare you the effort:

1. Bitcoin—Also known as BTC
2. Ether (not Ethereum)—Also known as ETH
3. Umm… That's not a crypto asset. That's just most of us trying to think of something here, and that, right there, is the problem.

We have mainly heard of these two cryptos, and rightfully so because both BTC and the ETH are giants. If you were to take these out of the equation, the crypto market would fall drastically, and I mean far more drastically than the stock markets fell in 2008.

As of the same date mentioned above, the total market cap of all the 7,000 or so cryptocurrencies accounted for $324.716 billion, and that number has gone on to climb significantly higher. Why am I so confident in saying that? Bitcoin, which happens to hold the biggest market cap of them all, alone holds a market cap of $945,984,123,929 as of December 8, 2021, and the total market cap of the entire crypto assets stands at a whopping $2.37 trillion (CoinMarketCap, 2021).

I will give you a moment to soak that information in. Once you are ready, we will proceed with the rest of the chapter where we will discover some of the most in-demand crypto assets as well as some interesting ones that are not very well known, at least not yet. I promise you; your list of 'Cryptos I should consider' is about to grow larger.

BTC vs ETH—The Battle of Giants

Let's start with the most obvious choices of them all. Whenever you browse a marketplace, you will always see these two popping up. Every marketplace takes pride in reflecting the fact that they allow BTC and ETH trades. Of course, they would! That's where most of the money is. However, the question here is why. Why is it that these two are the leading names in the world of cryptocurrencies? Why is it that they are on a massive upward trend that just does not seem to stop year after year? To learn that, let's dive into some details about both of these before we move on.

Bitcoin

Every cryptocurrency on the market comes bearing an official document called 'White paper.' It is this document that explains what a specific cryptocurrency is used for, what technology it uses, and all other relevant details that one may need to come to an informed decision. Bitcoin is no different as it, too, has a white paper.

According to its own white paper, BTC is a 'Peer-to-peer electronic cash system.' It is a revolutionary concept and a medium of exchange where the anonymity of the sender and the receiver is of the utmost importance.

The Limited Supply

The algorithms used to drive this cryptocurrency are smart and extremely complex. It is through this algorithm that new BTCs are awarded to computer users, or miners, who use their computing prowess to solve complex mathematical equations. We don't need to go into the specifics of what these issues are right now. All you need to know is that the number of BTCs in circulation continues to increase every day through a process called bitcoin mining. (I do have another book on cryptocurrency mining, which I recommend you pick up as well) This will remain true until the final BTC is mined, after which no more BTC can be mined.

When something as valuable as BTC is limited, in terms of total supply, investors can rest themselves assured that once the final BTC is mined, the prices of each BTC will sky-rocket. Some say it would be worth $1 million apiece while others argue it would easily break the $10 million barriers per BTC. Saying that it would be an exponential gain is very much of an understatement here.

According to its founder, a person that goes by the pseudonym of Satoshi Nakamoto, the total number of BTCs to hit the market will be 21 million BTCs. As of today, 18,895,000 BTCs have been mined so far, leaving just 2,000,000 or so BTCs behind. At the rate these are being mined, it would be safe to assume that the final BTC would be mined in the coming years. This still leaves a lot of room for people to join in and cash in on the potential reward at stake.

The Value That Changes

Of course, the biggest attraction in BTC is the ever-fluctuating price, and that's actually a good thing. Unlike stocks and commodities that also fluctuate in prices, the BTC price is purely speculative in nature. Earlier, I mentioned that BTC is not a physical form of currency like a dollar bill. It is not valued against reserves of gold or anything as such. It is just priced by you and me, the market makers.

To put things into a clearer perspective, a $1 bill will always have the same value across the country or even the world. Its value is based on the federal reserves of the country and the face value the bill bears.

On the other hand, BTC is free from any intrinsic value. It is just a number that exists. This number, if the large part of the market agrees, is determined as the new value for BTC. If more people like it, and more people buy it, the price goes up. It is simple supply and demand. When demand is higher than supply, the price goes up. It is just like a property that you buy, own, and then sell at what you believe is the right price. There will always be someone out there who will be willing to pay you that money if your property is adored by many others. Bitcoin, as far as the market has shown, is adored by many, many people.

Standing Strong

Since cryptocurrencies are decentralized and not backed by any kind of government institution or central bank, they behave very differently to factors that would otherwise affect stocks, currency exchange rates, and so on. The same is the case for BTC. It is decentralized and is not at all affected by factors such as:

- Inflation rates
- Economic growth indicators
- Monetary policies
- General elections
- National debt reports

This is something that further assures investors that such events would not generally cause a panic in the market.

The Ideal Replacement for Money?

To be honest, you wouldn't be wrong to consider this as the next medium of exchange. For now, we rely on paper money, hoping that they will go on to retain their value over time. We place an unshakeable trust in the banks and the Fed to do their jobs and help us ensure that our savings go on to grow bigger. However, somewhere in 2008 and 2009, some of the biggest financial institutions and organizations failed completely. This wasn't a problem for the US alone as they failed globally. As a result, the entire world experienced a massive recession. It was here that the fragile nature of our so-called modern financial system was highlighted. This is where the world started seeking ways to decentralize these financial services as a way to restore faith and provide a better customer experience.

The stage was set for something revolutionary to come in and fill the void, and that is where the pioneer of the cryptocurrencies that we have come to know and love today came in. The world was introduced to Bitcoin.

I already spoke about how the initial phase wasn't really all joy and glee for BTC. It took some time to settle, but once it did, it has never looked back. This new system removed banks from the equation altogether. No longer did people have to worry about paying through their banks to other banks or initiate transfer requests that would take ages to be processed. Now, through the P2P (peer-to-peer) system, everything is just a few clicks away.

A ledger system was implemented to ensure that everything ran smoothly and that no one was defrauding others. This ledger system was called 'Blockchain' and it was this that ensured all records of all transactions were publicly stored. This meant that if I paid you with 1 BTC, and I had 10 BTCs in total, the same record would be reflected in millions of other copies of the same ledger. This made tampering with the records completely impossible. Furthermore, since anonymity was at its source, it meant you never had to reveal your identity to the other party or worry about having your data leaked to third-party marketing firms.

Many firms and organizations have actually integrated BTC as a valid payment option. Back in 2010, Papa John's ended up striking a deal of ordering two pizzas in exchange for 10,000 BTCs. Since then, May 22 has been celebrated as Bitcoin Pizza Day. Imagine just what this person would be going through after realizing just how much profits he threw away for just two pizzas back then. Of all, there was no way of knowing how valuable each BTC would become in the future. Today, those 10,000 BTCs would be worth $50,000 x 10,000, which equates to $500,000,000 or $500 million in total. In terms of gain, well, that's a 2,000,000,000% gain just after a decade.

With everything in mind, it's safe to say that BTC is here to stay and that it's on track to hit big milestones soon. As of December 8th, 2021, each BTC is being traded for $50,200.

Always Something for Everyone

In November 2021, BTC was on the verge of setting a new all-time high by crossing $70,000. However, it failed to do so. What followed was just another reminder of just how volatile this market is supposed to be. It fell from $68,000 to around $42,000. Now, before you go on to panic, let me be the first to tell you that this scenario is perfectly normal and not unexpected for savvy Bitcoin investors.

You see, such corrections are bound to happen in every market. You cannot expect an asset to go upward all the time. There will be times when many investors would think, 'You know what? I would like to sell today and collect that good-looking profit.' One by one, many go on to sell. When you sell a BTC, it re-enters the market. The supply increases by one, and the market rate fluctuates ever so slightly. However, when hundreds of thousands of investors do the same at the same time, the price of BTC starts trending downwards.

While investors flee from this, I actually see this as an opening for new investors to enter the BTC wave. Instead of buying at $70,000, you now have the option to buy the same asset for a lot less. If the price of your favorite burger drops by 30%, would you buy it? Of course! There is no denying that what goes up must come down, and what has come down, in this case, BTC will always go back up. You can have a fair amount of confidence that it will happen because as mentioned previously, the supply of bitcoin is limited.

In short, every spike in a price is an opening for someone to either buy or sell, depending on the kind of strategy you use and the eventual goals you have. However, it is worth noticing here that if BTC takes a nosedive, for any given reason, most of the cryptocurrencies follow suit as well. That is because BTC, as it so happens to be, holds a vast majority of the market cap. If BTC is affected, the rest of the market feels the impact as well. Simply put, if BTC isn't faring well, hold your assets or seek out buying opportunities.

BTC promises to be the future of money. While no one can be certain of whether or not the future will unfold that way, one thing is certain; BTC is definitely a contender. It is something that continues to fascinate investors and traders alike, thanks to its high demand and volatility.

Ethereum—The Next Best Bet

So, BTC promises to replace the landscape of financial transactions. Great... but then, what would ETH do? What will its function be?

While many believe that Ethereum is in direct competition with BTC to try and gain the top spot, the fact is that it really isn't. In fact, it never intended to compete with BTC in the first place. ETH has its own set of goals. Furthermore, unlike BTC, the ETH uses a completely different technology, hosts different features, and follows different protocols.

Yes, Ethereum is a decentralized blockchain that is powered by its native token called Ether token. The Ether token enables a user to perform transactions and earn interest on their holdings. This can be done through staking, storing non-fungible tokens, playing games, using social media, or trading cryptocurrencies. There are many other things on the Ethereum blockchain, but in the interest of not confusing you, I will keep it limited for now.

Ethereum works on what is called a 'proof-of-work' blockchain (PoW). As a matter of fact, Bitcoin's blockchain is based on 'proof-of-work' as well. While this is a great blockchain, it is slower, and it requires quite a bit of gas fees, which is a fancier way of saying, 'Hey! You're going to pay me XYZ for doing all that work for you, once it's done!' Because Ethereum was designed to have a lot more applications on it, there have been many more activities on Ethereum, with the gas fee becoming a bigger and bigger problem. PoW is also a problem for the environment, as a huge amount of energy is required to maintain the blockchain.

Ethereum has announced it would be launching a completely new blockchain network and that all its operations would move to 'proof-of-stake' (PoS), which will be known as Ethereum 2.0. This would be seen as a more environmentally friendly and scalable way of doing things.

You may have heard about DeFi or dApps. As it so happens, they are all a part of the current Ethereum network. DeFi, or decentralized finance, and dApps, or decentralized apps, are meant to be used as the next-generation tools for web 3.0. Ethereum is constantly working towards enhancing our web experiences and helping many, many developers to cash in on the opportunity that will surely arrive once we enter the third generation of web surfing and the internet itself. Promising? Very much so!

History of ETH

Ethereum was introduced to fill in a void left by BTC. The white paper for Ethereum was released by a man named Vitalik Buterin, a co-creator of the project, in 2013. It mentioned smart contracts, using better automated and immutable 'if/then' statements, and explained how it would help the development of many decentralized applications. Ironically, this isn't the first time dApps were created. They had actually existed before Ethereum came into view. Buterin knew that dApps had one massive problem—They were not interoperable. To him, it was a challenge that needed a solution, and he had brought in the answer. For him,

Ethereum was what the world needed to unify these dApps and allow them to run and interact with each other. This is where Ethereum 1.0 came into existence.

'Wait. I'm confused.'

Think about it as Apple's App Store. Apple's terms and policies govern the hundreds of thousands of apps available on that store, which contain the following rules and limits. Now, take away those rulesets and let the developers have the ability to enforce their own rules within dApps. Instead of one body, like Apple, to control and enforce regulations, a community holds the power to play the same role. If the community dislikes something or wishes to enforce something, it will be done. No questions asked.

Now, picture that and improve all of that with the advent of Ethereum 2.0. It is safe to assume that things are looking extremely bright for ETH.

The Numbers

At the time of writing this part, you can grab yourself one ETH for $4,388 each. To give you an idea of some historic numbers for this year, here's how it looked like for ETH so far:

- January: $737

- February: $1,314

- March: $1,417

- April: $1,919

- May: $2,772

- June: $2,705

- July: $2,274

- August: $2,530

- September: $3,430

- October: $3,001

- November: $4,288

From the looks of it, it is on a clear upward trajectory, and it isn't going to end any time soon.

Both Sounds Great! Which One Should I Invest In?

Well, that really comes down to what your idea of 'investing' is and what your goals are. If you are looking to be more of a trader and walk away with some profits every now and then, perhaps BTC would be a better choice of the two because of the wider fluctuations. If you are able to read the charts carefully and predict the price action movement with a good probability, you can make money even if the price dips, as long as you bid on-sell or short.

For long-term investors, both BTC and ETH are promising candidates. However, it would all come down to a few questions:

1. What is your plan for investing and holding your assets?
2. What kind of profits are you seeking? (Insane or realistic)
3. How much can you afford to lose?
4. Can you keep your emotions in check when times are tougher?

Based on the answers you come up with, you can either choose to invest in BTC, ETH, or even both. However, not everyone may be able to invest $50,000 right away to buy themselves one BTC. This is where ETH can often be the next best thing to buy and hold on to.

What If I Choose Neither?

BTC and ETH are both great investment opportunities. However, if you are new to the game and these don't suit your fancy, there are still a lot of opportunities for us to uncover from the 7,000 or so cryptocurrencies and find ourselves some other crypto assets that are actually interesting enough to consider investing into.

However, before you do go on to invest, there are a few things that you should keep in mind when searching for opportunities.

- Market cap
- The 24-hour trading volume
- All-time high and all-time low figures
- Supply (both total and circulating)
- Coin's/token's protocol or network (such as Ethereum Classic, Polygon, etc.)

For now, keep in mind that BTC and ETH aren't the only currencies that are related to their respective blockchain networks or technology. In fact, many others hail using these networks, mostly ETH. This also means that if you go on to invest in a crypto asset that is based on the ETH blockchain, it will always go up in value if ETH is gaining value, and it will always go down when ETH is going down.

With that said, let's move on to some other famous cryptocurrencies that I believe are worth your consideration:

Binance Coin (BNB)

Earlier, I mentioned the term 'Binance,' which happens to be both an exchange and a leading coin at the same time. Binance offers some of the finest crypto tradings and investing services to date. It allows you to stake coins (using your crypto holdings or coins to earn rewards, it is similar to earning interest from cash savings in a bank, or dividends from stock holdings), gain early access to news about upcoming cryptocurrencies, and it allows you to earn interest on your crypto holdings. At the same time, they also have their very own coin that is aptly named Binance Coin (BNB).

The Binance coin happens to hold the prestigious third place overall with a market cap of $99,145,011,478 at the time of writing this section. It would be safe to say that BNB has increased both in fame and market cap significantly quicker than any other cryptocurrencies out there. Furthermore, with a current value of $593, it is safe to assume that this may very well overtake ETH in the future.

BNB is on Binance's own blockchain network, separate from Bitcoin's and Ethereum. You can find out more by reading the whitepaper on their official website or by checking it out on coinmarketcap.com to learn more.

Side note: Always check for a crypto asset on CoinGecko or CoinMarketCap to ensure you get the full picture and learn any key facts about the coin.

Solana (SOL)

Ah, yes! Not so long ago, practically nobody knew what I was talking about when I mentioned that I invested in Solana. They would imagine I bought something in a city project called Solana while others would think it was a Ponzi scheme and that I was being scammed for my money. Obviously, neither of that turned out to be true.

With a total supply of 510,812,389, and a current price of $193, Solana has swung into action and has gone on to attract attention from investors across the globe. This is particularly interesting because Solana (SOL) started in 2021 with a price of $1.7 per SOL. That's a significant increase in terms of returns, and the profits continue to come forth. From the looks of it, SOL is promising to be a coin you would want to buy and hold for years to come if you are one of those who want to enjoy the BTC wave but missed the actual event.

SOL operates on a proof-of-history (PoH) blockchain network, making it quite different from either ETH or BTC. However, as I mentioned earlier, if the general sentiment of BTC is bearish, or downwards, or if the general cryptocurrency market is facing a hard time, SOL will most likely follow suit.

Ripple (XRP)

For investors that are looking for crypto assets that cost less than $1, this is one of them, and it looks very promising as well.

Ripple is rated as the 7th most valuable cryptocurrency, in terms of total market cap ($41,002,031,237) and is based on the Binance Smart Chain Network (BEP20), which also happens to be the one that BNB uses.

Ripple promises to be a reliable medium of exchange, with lower fees and aims to be a leading enterprise solutions provider.

At the time of writing this, 47.25 B coins are in circulation. Ripple has a total of 100 billion coins of supply, out of which 99,990,075,944 coins have already been mined, minted, or discovered. This means that ripple is a coin that can no longer be mined.

With an all-time high of $3.84 and a current price of $0.86, it is safe to assume that this coin will definitely retest lost grounds and climb higher. Furthermore, the demand for this coin, if increased, could send the prices through the roof. Is it a good buy? Definitely! However, do not expect this one to shower you with profits like BTC or some other crypto assets can.

Terra (LUNA)

Another crypto asset that has surfaced literally out of nowhere and gone on to secure the 10th position in terms of total market cap. At the time of writing this, one LUNA is being traded for $72.

LUNA has a circulating supply of around 381 million and has a total supply of 854 million coins. No information reflects the max supply cap as you can find for BTC and other coins, which leaves some room to speculate whether the developers would go on to increase the cap or limit it to the total number of coins as reflected under 'total supply.'

LUNA had a decent start where it had an all-time low of $0.1199 around two years ago. On December 5th, 2021, it reached an all-time high when LUNA was sold for $77.94. See the potential here? If you time your entries right, you can actually walk away with significant profits.

Dogecoin (DOGE)

Did you think I would leave out the two coins that have gone on to cause so much havoc and created such hype on social media? Obviously not. The first one of the two happens to be this one.

Based on the same BEP20 chain, this mineable currency continues to impress investors and traders alike. With a reasonable price of $0.1802 per piece, it is being hailed as the Bitcoin killer. Whether that happens to be true or not remains to be seen, but one thing is for certain, DOGE is here to stay.

Unlike any of the crypto assets I have mentioned above, this crypto asset has reached its total lifetime supply of 132.44 billion coins. All of them are currently under circulation, meaning that you cannot mine or find a new one of these. The coin had set an all-time high in May of 2021 and reflected a price of almost $0.70. This means that there is plenty of room for it to regain and for us to profit from.

Shiba Inu (SHIB)

I mentioned that DOGE was one of the two coins that caused such a ruckus over social media. The other one happens to be this meme coin named Shiba Inu (SHIB).

There is possibly no other cryptocurrency in existence that has received the kind of attention this crypto asset has received. With more than 1,000,000 holders (investors that prefer retaining their coins for longer durations), it is easily one of the most ambitious projects and holds significant potential for its future.

As of today, around 549 trillion SHIB are in circulation. Initially, this coin was bound to have a total lifetime supply of 1 quadrillion, but almost half of these were then burned. This means that now, the total lifetime supply of SHIB will stand at 589 trillion coins.

Here's the beauty, though, since its release, which was around a year ago, it has provided 2,297,648% ROI. It recently set an all-time high price of $0.00008845, meaning that even at that point in time, you could get millions of Shiba Inu coins for just $100.

Currently, Shiba is undergoing a massive sell-off pressure and has dropped all the way back to the $0.00003 zone, which happens to be the perfect buying zone for those who are hoping to hold on to these. It is speculated that SHIB will go on to hit $0.01 per SHIB in the next two to three years. If that is the case, your $100 today can equate to over $10 million in just two to three years. This meme coin is definitely worth your consideration.

Time for us to look into some lesser-known coins too and see if there are any that we can look into for potential opportunities and returns in the near future.

Cryptos Worth Considering

Before we move ahead, please note that there is never a guarantee for profitable trades or investment opportunities as there are far too many variables that can often change the dynamics of the market. It is the same with other commodities and stocks as well. With that said, please invest what you can afford to lose. Of course, my aim is to help you invest in all the right assets. However, should these assets be later affected by something outside my control, I cannot be blamed or held responsible for these. Always proceed at your own risk.

I needed to say that because there may be those who may think I hold some kind of a magic wand or a crystal ball that allows me to see in the future. I don't. I may be wrong, and that's a risk I am willing to take. With that said, everything you come across is based on my research at this point. These may change or may not change by the time you read this book, meaning that you will need to do a bit of analysis on your own to see what the situation is like when you are ready to start investing.

The following are the cryptocurrencies that are not known to most crypto investors or traders. Most of the exchanges may not have these but they still exist in the shadows. These are crypto assets that have failed to grab the attention of the masses but show true potential and promise. Some of these may have already been picked up by some more savvy investors, but they are generally still overshadowed by bigger cryptos with their bigger market caps.

Monero (XMR)

There was once a time when I was able to find software that allowed me to mine these. Back then, each one of these would cost around $1 to mine, and I thought to myself 'Pfft! What a waste of energy!' I take my words back. Today, one XMR costs $211, and that's not even an all-time high. The all-time high for XMR happens to be $517. That's just incredibly high.

As of today, XMR stands at half the value of its ATH (all-time high). This means that there is still plenty of room for us to profit from. If you are a long-term holder, this may just be something worth your time.

Decentraland (MANA)

Based on the Ethereum blockchain, this is one of the first few Metaverse cryptos to grace the market. Metaverse, or Meta for short, is the new name Mark Zuckerberg has decided to stick with for rebranding Facebook. The Metaverse is actually a virtual reality universe where you can live, socialize, communicate, buy, sell, play, and enjoy. In fact, you can set up shop there and sell digital services, and for that, you can either be paid in MANA or any other supported cryptocurrencies. Do you see where this is leading?

Since Facebook's name has been changed to Meta, it's clear that the Metaverse will be a significant focus for the corporation. When the metaverse becomes more and more mainstream, MANA as a metaverse crypto will see more usage. This can potentially boost MANA's value to a new high.

At the time of writing, one MANA costs around $3.77.

Gala (GALA)

Gala happens to be selling for $0.4898 per GALA, at the time of writing this. Furthermore, only 6.98 billion GALAs are in circulation, and the total lifetime supply happens to be 35 billion. There's plenty of room for this to jump and reach utterly absurd all-time highs, and if you have the patience, you might be able to cash out with a large profit.

If you would have bought GALA on December 28th, 2020, you would have made 324,258% profit as of today because back then, it was selling for only $0.000151.

LTO Network (LTO)

At this point, LTO is currently operating near its dynamic support. This holds historical importance for this coin because whenever it has touched its dynamic support line, it has always bounced back up. You can expect the price of this coin to trend back upwards if the support holds.

The LTO is ranked at 421 on CoinMarketCap, has a 24-hour trading volume of over $54 million, and a total market cap of $116 million. The LTO project has a total supply of 397,969,833 and so far, 297 million are part of the circulation supply. It is proving to be a safe bet and one that provides good returns too.

Other Crypto Assets to Consider

The following cryptocurrencies are worth looking into as well.

1. CELR
2. ZRX
3. BTT
4. STX
5. MFT
6. COS
7. LINA
8. ARPA

9. CHR
10. DAR
11. COCOS
12. CHESS
13. WTC
14. SLP
15. ANT
16. BZRX
17. REQ
18. IOTA
19. SAND
20. AR

You can browse for these or even find more that you may be interested in by going to coinmarketcap.com. One great way to know which cryptocurrencies are on the rise is by checking out various social media platforms, such as:

- Twitter
- Discord
- Facebook communities and pages
- Reddit

Seasoned traders and investors know and believe a quote that says 'The trend is your friend.' If something is trending, it is bound to give you great returns.

Now that you have learned 'some' possible cryptocurrencies that you can invest in or trade, the next obvious question would be:

'How on earth do we buy or sell cryptocurrencies?'

That is precisely what we will cover in the next chapter.

Chapter 8. Cryptocurrency Exchanges

The most well-known way of investing in cryptocurrencies is through an online cryptocurrency exchange, enabling the purchase, sale, and trade of cryptos for other cryptocurrencies for fiat money, such as the US dollar. It is also called a digital currency exchange or DCE. It facilitates the exchange of cash into cryptocurrencies and vice-versa.

Centralized Exchanges

These are like traditional stock exchanges. The exchange acts as a middleman between the buyer and the seller, and in exchange for these services, it charges transaction fees. Most centralized exchanges provide crypto-crypto pairings.

- A crypto-crypto pairing consists of exchanging one cryptocurrency for another.

- A fiat-crypto pairing involves exchanging a conventional currency for a cryptocurrency.

The primary issue with centralized cryptocurrency exchanges is that they are susceptible to hacks and scandals. Therefore, you must choose an exchange wisely.

Coinbase

This is the most widely used exchange across the world. It supports Bitcoin (BTC), Litecoin (LTC), Bitcoin Cash (BCH), and Ethereum (ETH). Among fiat currencies, investors can use the US dollar (USD), the Euro (EUR), and the British Pound (GBP).

Bittrex

This exchange supports the US dollar (USD), Bitcoin (BTC), Ethereum (ETH), Tether (USDT), and various other pairings.

Kraken

This exchange also has several pairings available on its website apart from the general US dollar (USD) and the euro (EUR).

Gemini

This New York-based exchange has great regulation benchmarks in the US. This exchange supports Bitcoin (BTC), Ethereum (ETH), Zcash (ZEC), and the US dollar (USD).

Bitfinex

This exchange requires a minimum of $10,000 equity to start trading. It also offers numerous fiat currencies like the US dollar (USD), the Japanese yen (JPY), the euro (EUR), and the British pound (GBP). Bitfinex charges an inactivity fee if you hold your balances and do not participate in the markets.

Binance

This exchange is one of the fastest rising and offers a mobile application.

Huobi

Huobi supports cryptocurrencies such as Tether (USDT), Bitcoin (BTC), Ethereum (ETH), and Huobi Token (HT). This exchange is not available for investors in the US because of some government policies.

KuCoin

This is also a centralized exchange that supports multiple cryptocurrencies on its platform.

Decentralized Exchanges

These exchanges do not rely on middlemen to carry out transactions. A decentralized cryptocurrency exchange (DEX) is a platform where buyers and sellers come together and execute the transactions between each other.

On these exchanges, you will be able to contact other investors and buy and sell cryptos directly from them. You can utilize options like smart contracts and atomic swaps to carry out the deals. Since cryptocurrencies became popular because of their decentralized structure, some market participants believe that using decentralized exchanges makes more sense.

Though decentralized exchanges are less vulnerable to hacks than centralized ones, they do have some other issues particular to this type of exchange. With decentralized exchanges, you are more likely to lock yourself out of access to your money. If you lose your login details, you may end up being locked out of your own account as the system may mistake you for a hacker. Other issues faced by these exchanges are low volumes and low liquidity. Apart from this, most centralized exchanges do not offer benefits to deposit or withdraw fiat currencies.

IDEX

It is a decentralized exchange for trading Ethereum (ETH) tokens. It is pretty much the most user-friendly exchange and can connect to your digital wallet without any hassles.

Waves DEX

Waves DEX supports multiple cryptocurrencies such as Bitcoin (BTC), Ethereum (ETH), Litecoin (LTC), Monero (XMR), and several other cryptos, including the exchange's own crypto token, Waves (WAVES). On this exchange, you can trade fiat currencies as well.

Stellar DEX

This exchange allows you to trade Bitcoin (BTC), Ethereum (ETH), Litecoin (LTC), Ripple (XRP) in addition to the fiat currencies like the US dollar (USD), Japanese yen (JPY), etc.

Bisq DEX

This exchange is based on a peer-to-peer system. You can trade several cryptocurrencies on this platform, and you can also exchange fiat currencies like dollars, euros, or yen.

Hybrid Exchanges

These exchanges incorporate the benefits of both centralized and decentralized exchanges, so the users get the best of both worlds. They merge the functionality and liquidity of a centralized exchange with the privacy and security of a decentralized exchange. Hybrid exchanges are believed to be the future of cryptocurrency exchanges.

Hybrid exchanges seek to facilitate cryptocurrency investment with the speed, comfort, and liquidity consumers are used to in conventional exchanges. It attaches its centralized elements to a network of decentralized elements.

Hybrids are also known as semi-decentralized exchanges because they integrate on-chain as well as off-chain elements. An off-chain transaction shifts the value of your cryptocurrency outside of the blockchain.

Qurrex was the first-ever hybrid exchange. It was launched in 2018. The Qurrex team was formed in 2016, and it included experts who were experienced in trading in the foreign exchange, trade terminal developers, and creators of stock and futures exchanges. They collectively decided that there was considerable potential in involving the best methods and procedures of the traditional exchanges to develop a new cryptocurrency exchange incorporating the centralized and decentralized elements.

Choosing an Exchange

As you must have noticed in the previous sections of this chapter, there is no shortage of cryptocurrency exchanges in the market. And with the growth of cryptocurrency, other varieties of exchange are bound to be developed. This confuses beginners, and they stress about which exchange they should choose.

There are a few characteristics you can go through so that you make a sound decision and choose a cryptocurrency exchange that works best for you. The following sections mention these factors:

Security

The cryptocurrency exchanges are at perpetual risk of hacks, scams, and frauds. This is the reason it is advisable to do your research before choosing an exchange. Online reviews on sites such as Reddit or news organizations like Forbes are some of the places you can visit to help you choose a safe and secure platform to trade crypto. Mentioned below are the other factors you must consider checking about your cryptocurrency exchange:

- **Two-factor authentication:** This is a strategy used to confirm the identity you are claiming by combining two factors. The first thing the cryptocurrency exchange knows, for example, is your login password, and this is something it sends by mail or phone to complete the second step of verification.

- **Cold storage:** An exchange is providing cold storage means that it is storing your funds offline so that the risk of online hacking is managed.

Supported Currencies

When you have chosen the cryptocurrency, you want to invest in, you must ensure that the chosen exchange carries that respective coin. In addition to this, if you are a beginner in the market, you will presumably need an exchange that permits you to deposit your country's fiat currency. Some exchanges use only cryptocurrencies, while others allow the use of fiat currencies as well.

Fees

Cryptocurrency exchanges charge their users in various ways because that is the only way they make money. They charge their customers transaction, deposit, and withdrawal fees. The amount of fees charged differs from exchange to exchange. In some exchanges, a sliding scale decreases the fee percentage as the customer's trading volume rises.

Location

Depending on your location, you may come across a cryptocurrency exchange that works better for you than any other, more popular one on an international level does.

Also, the location of the exchange decides the laws it has to follow. Several countries still do not have any particular regulations regarding cryptocurrencies. But if and when they dictate certain regulations, it may affect your potential to participate in the crypto market through these exchanges.

Payment Methods

While researching the exchanges, make sure that you look into the modes of payment acceptable to the exchange. Different exchanges use different methods. Some require deposits by bank transfer, some use PayPal, some take credit and debit cards. Generally, the easier it is for you to pay, the more fees you will be charged because the exchanges will make you pay for ease or convenience of use.

Brokers

If you only want to speculate the price action of cryptocurrencies and not invest in them online, you may want to consider using brokers.

As cryptocurrencies gained popularity, some Forex currency brokers began providing their services as brokers. But do understand that you cannot buy cryptocurrencies from a broker. All they are doing is furnishing a tradable price on their platform. That way, investors may benefit from the market volatility and earn or lose money, depending on how they speculate.

Traditional Forex brokers are the intermediaries between a trader and networks of big banks. These brokers generally get a price from one or more than one bank for a particular currency. They then offer the investor the best price they have obtained from their banks. The investors can then trade their chosen currencies based on streaming prices on the broker's platform.

These brokers work on something known as the over-the-counter (OTC) markets. This shows that cryptocurrencies are traded through a network of dealers instead of a centralized exchange.

Brokers earn money primarily through commission fees. Some of them may make money even when their customers lose capital. This is one of the reasons the Forex industry started earning a bad reputation.

Pros of Using a Broker

The brokers are able to provide increased liquidity to their customers because they get their quotes from multiple exchanges. This means that you may get your orders executed within a stipulated time and may also get a very close price to your original orders because the broker has more than one channel to find a buyer or seller to complete your order. Also, with almost all brokers, you can get your account confirmation quicker than when you use an exchange.

Cons of Using a Broker

While trading in the cryptocurrency market using a broker, you do not own your coins because you are just speculating on the market's price action rather than actually purchasing cryptocurrency. Additionally, you do not have a portfolio or a wallet.

Chapter 9. Cryptocurrency Trading Strategies and Tactics

Tips for Picking Your Winning Strategy

Investing in digital currency is a great way to make some money, no matter who you are. And even though the demand for some digital currencies is high right now, this is still just the beginning, and you can still get in relatively early. Other companies that have seen this kind of growth are now big names that are expensive to purchase and won't make as much profit unless you have a lot to start. But digital currencies are still rising and will continue to grow.

With that being said, it is a good idea to have a strategy to help you get the results needed for success with digital currencies. It is not enough to just put your money into the market and hope that it all works out well for you. This might work right now while the market is doing well for some people, but you have to remember that investing in the cryptocurrency market is just like any other investment.

At some point, these digital currencies will start to stabilize some more, and, depending on how various governments around the world start reacting to these coins, some of them may begin to fall. Having a good strategy in place can help protect you if this starts to happen, making sure that you still get out of the market with a profit, even if the market ends up spiking back down.

As a beginner, you may be uncertain about the steps you should take to pick a good strategy and see the results you want, no matter which digital currency you decide to go with. All of them work similarly, and you will be able to use this information to help you pick out the winning strategy you want. Whether you are working with smart contracts, day trading, the 'buy and hold' strategy, or another option, it is crucial to have a plan in place.

Pick a Good Currency

When looking into this kind of investment, you should first pick out the right type of currency. There are thousands of these currencies available for you to choose from, and not all of them will do all that well when you get started. All of these cryptocurrencies can't do well in the market; some will keep on going, and some are going to fail pretty quickly. You want to choose a digital currency that is likely to succeed, one that will last a long time and earn you money.

Bitcoin is a great example, but you need to be careful with getting oversaturated too quickly. There are also a lot of other cryptocurrencies that are not as well-known but will be able to make you some good money in the long run if you give them time and invest in them the proper way.

The most important thing to remember is to conduct thorough research. Each digital currency will have its own market and operate in a unique way. You want to make sure that you research how to invest in a given digital currency and even the type of exchange it is traded on to determine if it will stay around for long or not.

There are a lot of exceptional digital currencies out there that you can use. Bitcoin is a popular option, but there are many other options you can go with, and since they are not as popular and well-known, they can sometimes provide you with the most return on investment. No matter which digital currency you would like to work with, it is essential to do your research ahead of time to pick out an excellent option that will last for a long time, continue to grow, and make you money.

Remember that thousands of digital currencies are available on the market. Many developers are hoping to create a currency that will take off and will earn them some money in the process. But the market is just not big enough for thousands of currencies to survive. However, just because these currencies are not big names doesn't mean that they aren't profitable. Stick with your strategy.

There are a lot of great plans that you can choose when this comes to investing in the digital currency market. All of them can help you make some good money, but you need to follow a few rules to get the most out of your work.

The worst thing that you can do when working with a strategy that you pick is to get into a trade and then switch up plans. This is common with beginners who see that their investment is not doing all that well in the market, and they want to change things, or perhaps they don't understand the strategy they are working with, so they make mistakes. Before you pick out a good plan, make sure that you go through and fully understand the rules that go with each strategy. And then, when you get into the market, make sure that you keep with that same strategy until the trade is made.

Learn How to Keep the Emotions Out

No matter what kind of investment you choose to go with, it is essential that you never let your emotions get in the way. You can be the most level-headed person in the world, someone who usually thinks through their decisions and makes sure that they are doing what is best for their money, but trading and investing can mess with the emotions. As soon as those emotions get in the way, you are going to end up with problems.

If your emotions get in the way, this is a lot harder to think through decisions. You may get caught up in the market and may make split-second decisions that are not the best for you just because they may have made sense at the moment. Your emotions may make you stay in the market too long and cause you to lose a lot more money than if you had just placed your stops in place and stuck with them. Or your emotions may get in the way when you are making money, and you will end up losing money because you couldn't just take your profits and walk, and you end up staying in the market until it starts going down.

This is why this is so important to come up with a strategy and then stick with it. You'll be able to stick to the rules that come with that plan and make important judgments without allowing emotions to get in the way. These strategies help you to get decisions made long before you even get into the market. Then, no matter how the market behaves, you will be able to make a trade and get out of the market without emotions getting in the way.

Use Your Stop Points and Don't Deviate

Stop points are the two points when you exit the market, no matter how well or poorly the market ends up doing later. Sometimes, in the heat of the trade, you may be tempted to stay in longer than your stop points, but these are meant to help lessen your risk and to keep your profits as high as possible.

This is going to be the point where you will get out of the market and just accept your losses if the investment reaches this point. No one wants to take on a loss, but a stopping point is essential because this keeps emotions out of the game. If you see that the stock is going down, you may panic and make decisions that are not best.

This is common for some beginners to get caught up in the whole trade that they are working. You may think that you can stay objective, that you will be able to make the right decisions no matter what, but when you see that the market is starting to go down and that your investment is not doing well, will you be able to stay as an objective in the long run? Most new investors will see the numbers going down, and they will hold onto the stock, hoping that it will rebound again and make money back. The issue here is that sometimes the market will not bounce, and if you keep the money in the market, you may find that you lose out on more than you can afford in the long run.

Setting the stop point is essential to limit the amount of loss that you may incur. You should set a stop at the point where you would be comfortable losing that much money if the market turned. Right now, the market is doing well, but this is best to plan so that you don't lose out on more money than you can afford.

Also, you need to make sure that you are setting a stopping point for profits gained. With how much the market is going up, this may seem a little silly, but it is still a good thing to have in place. You should withdraw at this point, considering the advantage that you earn. You can always get back into the market, but this option ensures that you do not stay for so long that the market turns, and you lose all of your profits.

Stay Anonymous on These Networks

While the blockchain is a pretty secure piece of technology that helps build trust in the system and keep your information pretty safe, this is a good idea to keep your data as private and anonymous as possible. You will have to give up some personal information on most exchange sites now, especially if you live in the United States, but outside of that, there are some ways to remain anonymous.

First, when picking out the address you want to use on these networks, do not use your personal information. Placing your first and last name as the address just opens you up to others finding your data quickly. It will not take a hacker long to see what transactions you have completed and how much you earned in the process. They would then be able to use that information to find your account, make money, or perform identity fraud.

Besides, it is best not to give your name out to others on the network. Your address should be enough, and if you picked out the right kind, this should not have any of your personal identification information. These networks also don't have any screening options, and they are not there to protect you at all. This implies that if you're not careful, you risk giving your personal information to someone who will make money off of it.

Always be careful with who you are talking to online on digital currency networks, and make sure that you keep your personal information safe. Most retailers and others you may be working with will be happy just receiving your unique address to complete the transaction. If someone asks for more information than that, you should remember that your anonymity is important online and keep that information to yourself.

Store Your Coins in Cold Storage

You must have a few different storage methods for keeping your coins as safe as possible. There are a lot of hackers and scammers out there who would love nothing more than to get into your account and just take the coins. And since digital currencies do not work the same as the big banks or other financial institutions that you usually operate with, if the money disappears and you don't have a backup to prove the coins belong to you, you are just out of luck.

You have the potential to make a lot of money when you are working with digital currencies. Depending on what strategy you use and how well the market is doing, you can easily double, triple, or more your money in a short amount of time.

No matter what form of investing you choose to conduct, the type of storage you employ is critical. Also, keep your key up to date regularly. As you earn more coins or use some of the coins, you need to make sure to update your key with this information to get the exact amount back into your account if something goes wrong.

Ask For Advice From a Broker When Needed

No matter how much you research the niche of digital currencies, there is still going to be a lot that you can learn. It is much better to ask questions than ignore them and hope they are not a big deal. The digital currency market is great to get into right now, but it is volatile and could turn around any day. At the very least, consider finding a friend or someone who has worked in the market for some time who would be happy to answer your questions and help you get along in this kind of market.

Working with digital currencies is a great way to put your money to work for you. There are many digital currencies out there right now that you can choose to work with, which gives you a lot of opportunities to pick from for your investment. Follow some of these tips before you get started to ensure that you are making the right decisions and making a good profit when trading in digital currencies.

Chapter 10. The Future of Cryptocurrency

By now, you must have many ideas about cryptocurrencies in your mind. But you might just be wondering where to begin. I would suggest you observe the existing conditions and opportunities around you and then analyze where you stand. But after coming this far, are you just wondering if crypto trading is worth it? Are you curious about the future of cryptocurrency? Do you think that ever since its introduction to the world about a decade ago, cryptocurrency has made its mark with a groundbreaking innovation?

The Future of Bitcoin

Bitcoin's future appears to be both unforeseeable and unstoppable. Nobody knows what will happen, but Bitcoin appears to have made such inroads into the mainstream that it will be impossible to reverse. Numerous major businesses, including airlines, technology businesses, government organizations, and the financial industry, have begun to embrace Bitcoin and, perhaps more significantly, the underlying blockchain technology. Moreover, the growing demand for skilled blockchain programmers across various businesses demonstrates the blockchain era.

A new generation of entrepreneurs has emerged in the cryptocurrency and blockchain area, inventing novel applications centered on Bitcoin as both a currency and a technology. Only time will tell if Bitcoin as a currency will continue to appreciate and continue to dominate the cryptocurrency markets or whether a disruptive upstart will dethrone it. Diversifying your cryptocurrency holdings is viewed as a technique to boost your chances of picking a winner by many.

Hearing stories about early Bitcoin adopters who made millions can make people to Bitcoin feel as if they are too late. While it is unknown whether Bitcoin will be the 'one coin to rule them all,' the promise of blockchain technology is only just beginning to gain traction in the mainstream, bubbling to the surface of a vast sea of possibility. No crystal ball can reveal the precise shape of the future, but one thing is certain: this is only the beginning. Five or ten years from now, people who invest prudent investments today may very well be considered 'early adopters.'

The Future of Ethereum

Ether's value reached all-time highs in 2021, and many believe that the value will continue to rise over time. Numerous large companies have embraced Ethereum's promise of a scalable blockchain platform capable of executing smart contracts. As the promise of blockchain technology becomes more apparent on a global scale, a wave of entrepreneurs has emerged to incorporate it into every field of technology, from energy to healthcare to politics.

It remains to be seen whether the Ethereum platform will ultimately become the de facto foundation for developing decentralized blockchain apps. Ethereum could be compared to an early web browser such as Netscape Navigator, and some future attempt could become the 'Google of blockchain.' Given the novelty of this technology, it would be naive to dismiss that possibility. But, of course, Ethereum may continue to grow, improve, and ultimately dominate this space. The imminent switch to the Casper algorithm and proof-of-stake will be a litmus test for Ethereum's ability to evolve.

Whether you intend to invest in Ether or another token produced via an Ethereum-based application, or you wish to develop your decentralized application on the Ethereum blockchain, it is critical to keep informed. Technology advances at a breakneck pace in this space, and when blockchain technology penetrates large businesses, we will certainly see changes in the way cryptocurrencies and blockchain applications are regulated. Joining online groups and conversations like Reddit, Slack channels, and Twitter is an excellent way to remain informed about Ethereum platform advancements. Learning about other platforms, reading whitepapers, and becoming acquainted with how leaders in this field can help you develop a broader perspective. A deeper understanding can help you formulate your own opinions about which technologies are likely to succeed and how to invest.

Of course, we cannot predict how the future will unfold. But, regardless of how the future unfolds, it is almost destined to be shaped by blockchain technology. Today, Ethereum represents one of the most established and forward-thinking approaches to making this technology accessible, adaptable, and exciting. As a result, the opportunities are limitless for investors, developers, and entrepreneurs in this cutting-edge space.

Let us look at a case scenario to understand how Ethereum can benefit enterprises. Robert is an entrepreneur in the finance sector. Recently, Robert shifted all of his company's transactions to Ethereum. He says that cryptocurrency helps in business payment settlements while maintaining high privacy and upgrading his business performance. In addition, Robert anticipates that the next decade will be an era of low-cost and high-speed payments due to the increased use of Ethereum and other such cryptocurrencies in businesses.

The Future of Blockchain

Throughout this book, we have discussed various fundamental principles relating to blockchain technology. As the world becomes more connected via networked technology and the amount of data, we generate increases quantity and quality, there is a rising demand and opportunity for new organizational structures to manage the interface between digital and material life. The use of a distributed ledger in conjunction with the ability to create decentralized rather than hierarchical systems in a safe, trustless, and open manner is a significant step toward reinventing how many of today's dominating institutions operate.

As with any new technology, the blockchain ecosystem is characterized by opposing philosophies, disparate implementations, and a slew of obstacles. Only time will tell if the Bitcoin blockchain will remain the dominant blockchain model and Bitcoin will remain the most popular cryptocurrency. Without question, there is a tremendous opportunity for growth to reach the full potential of blockchain technology in terms of institutional transparency, decentralized networks, peer-to-peer transactions, and asset management, to name a few. Healthcare, banking, social media, retail, aviation, and manufacturing have all begun to investigate the feasibility of integrating with blockchain-based systems. Governments, banks, and nonprofit groups have already begun implementing blockchain technology to govern transactions, public service access, and humanitarian aid distribution.

Executing transactions in a trustless environment without using a 'middleman' is a basic tenet of blockchain technology. In layman's terms, we ultimately trust an unbiased mathematical process performed by computers rather than human individuals. As a result, we are assured of a level of security that is theoretically impervious to human meddling.

In fact, it is difficult to disregard human beings fully. The strength of a decentralized application based on computational verification represents a paradigm shift away from a top-down structure and toward a distributed network. However, a closer examination of the Bitcoin blockchain reveals that the consensus model requires agreement by a majority to verify a block. A majority of miners (51%).

What if, as mining costs continue to rise in tandem with the ever-growing blockchain, miners consolidate their influence into ever-larger pools? This is not a purely theoretical matter. At the time of this writing, two big mining pools are expected to mine about 50% of all Bitcoin blocks.

To execute a so-called '51 percent attack,' a single organization must provide at least 51% of the Bitcoin network's mining hash rate. This would take an almost unfathomable amount of computer power, equating to an equally unfathomable electrical cost. In reality, most governments lack the resources necessary to execute a 51 percent attack on Bitcoin. It would be extremely tough, but not impossible. If this were to occur, the attacker would be unable to gain complete control of the network. Instead, they would prevent new transactions from being validated but not reverse previously recorded transactions, take Bitcoins from other people's wallets, or produce new Bitcoins at will.

The 51% issue is one that any decentralized system created on a similar model would face. However, according to certain proponents of the proof-of-stake consensus, this model provides stronger security against a 51 percent attack.

Blockchains, like other burgeoning industries and new technologies, confront obstacles. However, the blockchain space is generating a whole generation of entrepreneurs, developers, and experts. It is a country of opportunity for individuals who believe in the technology's transformative potential.

Whether you are intrigued by the ideological implications of decentralized networks fundamentally altering the landscape of hierarchical organizations on a global scale or are an investor looking for the next big thing, blockchain technology is undeniably intriguing. Without a doubt, blockchain is the way of the future. Despite a surge in interest in blockchain technology over the last few years, we are still in the very early phases of this field. Even if you are unfamiliar with blockchain technology now, in five or ten years, you will almost certainly be deemed an 'early adopter' of the most disruptive technology since the Internet's inception.

Risk and Money Management

Money management is almost certainly the most critical idea in investing. If you lack a professional way to calculate the lot size, regardless of your trading technique, your account will be a non-starter. I am hoping that we can figure out how to calculate your risks together. Therefore, carefully examine the primary money management guidelines that I define for the cryptocurrency market.

10% of the risk in a single trade: That is, if you make a single trade, you will bear no more than 10% of the risk. If you make five trades each day, divide 10% of your risk by. Avoid numerous transactions in an attempt to increase your earnings. Paying commission fees to the exchange will cost you a lot of money.

30% of cash in the account should always be the bare minimum: Never invest entirely in cryptocurrencies or fiat currency. Even if the currency's value decreases, you should retain some cryptocurrency assets. Accordingly, when the market grows, you should hold fewer Bitcoins and more Ether and altcoins. The greater an asset's capitalization, the less volatile it is. Thus, if you desire less volatility in the fall, keep a portion of your funds in Bitcoin. Although 10%–20% of your total funds should be kept in cash, you should not retain everything in cash. If you own Bitcoin, you can buy altcoins, as they are frequently exchanged for Bitcoin. Simultaneously, you should have at least 30% of the cash on hand, especially during periods of rapid market expansion. You may require funds for a new intriguing Initial Coin Offering (ICO), a new altcoin movement, or something else.

The rationale for entry and exit should be identical: When you enter a trade, you should have an exit strategy in mind. Any scenario should have an exit strategy. All of your plans should be laid out in detail on paper, and you should not abandon them.

Diversifying markets and assets: If you are going to trade, you should do so on at least two respected exchanges. Take no risks, even if the newly opened exchange entices you with low fees or a bounty.

Make few trades and abstain from gambling: Here, you must determine the frequency with which you access the terminal and monitor the quotes. I advocate monitoring cryptocurrency activity no more than once a day. To complete this task, choose a time of day when you are most relaxed. For instance, you arrive home from work, pour a glass of red wine (or a cup of tea), and sit down peacefully to check on the latest developments in the cryptocurrency market. You do not need to obsessively monitor the market every ten minutes. This type of neurotic behavior is detrimental to both your health and your bank account.

Have your own perspective and do not succumb to peer pressure: No one on the planet can tell you with certainty how much Bitcoin will cost tomorrow or make other accurate predictions. As a result, if you hear highly publicized projections in favor of a particular coin, this individual is almost certainly prejudiced in some way.

I remind you once again that nothing is definite. I recommend that you maintain a healthy skepticism at all times. Nobody knows what the future holds. Keep this in mind and you will see right through the scam. If someone persuades you of something, consider why this man is so adamant in proving his position. You can listen to other people's opinions, but you cannot invest in being guided by them.

Keep the stop orders in mind: As previously said, stop orders make no sense in the cryptocurrency market because they may not work or may perform poorly. As a result, always keep your stop (exit point) in mind or record it in a notepad. For instance, I purchased Ether for $250 to liquidate the position at $200.

After reading this book, I'm sure you've learned how risky the bitcoin market is. However, you will not be able to earn such gains anywhere else. Nowhere else in the world is it possible to double or triple an amount in a single day.

Finally, I want to emphasize that nothing is certain in the cryptocurrency market. If someone makes a guarantee to you, that person is a liar. Prepare for this, as similar scenarios occur frequently in this market. The most cunning and astute individuals (creators of initial coin offerings, experienced traders, and so on) compete in the cryptocurrency market, each pursuing their own objectives.

Investment Strategies

Would you rather make profits off your cryptocurrencies simply by purchasing Bitcoins or embrace more complex ideas? In the previous chapters of this book, I provided you with scenarios about how some of my students and friends accomplished their crypto goals. Surely, they all followed some of the most suitable investment strategies. It is vital to look at your chances of success while opting for a certain strategy.

Before going right to the strategies, you can employ in your cryptocurrency trading, let us have a look at the two major types of trading you can do in the current market.

Margin Trading

Margin trading is straightforward. You trade borrowed money. You pay a portion of the stock price (called the margin) and borrow the rest from other market participants who are ready to lend you money when you buy on margin. Your margin account balance is used just to represent this borrowed money and, if necessary, to cover loan expenses. In other words, margin trading enables you to trade with money that you do not possess. Leverage refers to the borrowed capital used in trade.

Assume that you have $10,000. It is, in a sense, your margin. Assume you choose to trade with a leverage of 1:4. This allows for a $40,000 transaction. Your profit margin is 25%. You buy for $40,000, and if the purchased currency increases in value, your profit increases fourfold. However, if the purchased currency decreases in value, your losses increased fourfold as well. Thus, if you buy $10,000 in cryptocurrencies, you risk losing all of your money only if the value of your asset (for example, Bitcoin) falls to zero. However, if you invest $40,000 in cryptocurrencies using leverage on a margin account, you will lose all of your personal funds ($10,000) if the asset falls by 25%.

Consider another scenario: you maintain a margin position in Ether during a flash drop. In this situation, the exchange will close your position because Ether had fallen more than 25% at the time. As soon as your loss reaches $10,000, the stock exchange will close your position at $40,000 in value. That is, $10,000 serves as collateral for your trade.

Margin or leverage is an excellent instrument for enhancing your profit in any other market. Almost every seasoned trader takes advantage of leverage. However, as previously said, the bitcoin market is extremely volatile, so leverage can literally destroy you. Why does this occur? Consider the stock market.

What could possibly cause Apple's stock to fall by, say, 20%? Nothing of the sort could happen, in my opinion. As a result, it is generally safe to trade Apple stock using leverage, as the stock cannot fall by more than 10% in a single day. Simultaneously, you can always take a position in the stock market, as trade is strictly controlled, and you can keep track of all happenings.

In contrast, the cryptocurrency market is open 24 hours a day, seven days a week.

Even the most illogical and nonsensical outcome is possible here because the price can increase or decrease by any proportion. As a result, if you are going to trade on margin in the bitcoin market, you would be wise to utilize a leverage ratio of 1:2. Leveraged trading is akin to Russian roulette. Your position will almost certainly be ruined if you trade with a leverage of 1:4.

Always exercise caution: if you come across an exchange with a questionable interface or are offered 1:20 leverage, the exchange will likely look for marginal traders. It is on the lookout for greedy, crafty, and, as practice demonstrates, foolish traders looking to double their earnings instantly. As a result, let me reiterate that you should be verified on the leading exchanges if you choose to trade professionally. You should open at least two accounts for each of them.

You should have two margin accounts: one for your money and one for margin. To begin trading with leverage, you should move funds from your primary account to a margin account, from which you can trade.

Additionally, you should be familiar with the following aspects of margin trading. Do you believe you will be compensated for trading in money for nothing more than a 'thank you?' Not. You will only be provided interest-bearing money. If you use 1:4 leverage and wish to trade $40,000 rather than $10,000, you will pay a higher interest rate. It can reach 1% to 2% per day. Interest accrues to a total of $30,000 in the matter at hand. I would want to remind you that you only have $10,000.

Finally, here are some beginner tips:

- When you trade the market, you acquire assets whose value has plummeted precipitously. This is my principal strategy at the moment: to buy assets that are cheap or whose values have plummeted.

- To close a position, place an order only if you have earned a profit of at least 50%. Waiting for higher profits is extremely dangerous, so close your position immediately after earning your 50%. Additionally, I do not advocate earning less than 10% profit. To my mind, 20% is the bare minimum you should aim for. However, if you engage in intraday trading, you may put sell orders at 30%+.

- Bear in mind that the exchange charges a commission. The fewer trades you make, the greater the costs. And when your revenue increases, your commission rates decrease.

Day Trading and Long-Term Position Trading

Let us concentrate on your job schedule at the Bitcoin exchange.

Before you begin trading, you must make a critical decision on how much time you are willing to devote to trading. Of course, the optimal solution is to spend 5-6 hours a day at the computer, continually closing positions and monitoring the situation. However, due to a lack of time, the bulk of people today opt for a different option. They trade goods once a week. On a given day, such traders review the week's news and any charts and then determine which positions to open or close.

Many individuals choose this route. Therefore, here are some pointers:

- Choose one day of the week that you will devote exclusively to trading.

- On this day, examine your portfolio to determine which currencies have increased in value and which have decreased in value.

Keep an eye on the news. Make judgments based on current events and the mix of your portfolio. If the value of an asset has not increased or has even decreased, close the position. If you see anything that appears to be promising or is on price, buy it. You should do these transactions on each day of the week that you have designated for trading. By the way, I propose Blockfolio as a more convenient way to track your positions.

To summarize, I recommend one of the two approaches to trading: daily monitoring with limited sell orders or weekly monitoring.

Simultaneously, certain cryptocurrency exchanges, such as Bitfinex, provide OTC trading. The abbreviation OTC stands for Over the Counter, which refers to a transaction that occurs over the counter. This is a decentralized market that lacks a central physical location and in which market participants trade assets via the dealers' network.

For instance, if you lack time to monitor the market and are completely focused on trading via order placement, you can utilize the services of this market. Your cooperation will be conducted over the phone or by e-mail. Thus, you inform a trader that you wish to buy 250 bitcoins. After perusing the market, the dealer determines how much you should pay for this number of bitcoins. For this service, the dealer will charge a fee.

Below are some of the crypto investment strategies:

Buy Bitcoin

As a result of this method, all you need to do is to purchase Bitcoin. This technique is optimal in every way. It is straightforward to apply, and you will not be required to delve into the complexities of economic or technical principles. As a result, this method may yield the greatest profit.

Follow the Money

Here, I recommend that you purchase a set number of different coins from the top ten greatest cryptocurrencies available today.

In other words, you will acquire several market leaders. The coins, whose value would surge, will compensate for the losses incurred due to the failure of the other coins. Additionally, this technique entails enormous risks.

Nothing can shield you from the reality that coins that have appeared to be stable in the past year may experience a significant decline in value next year. However, you should keep in mind that there are currently no fundamental reasons for Bitcoin to fail, which could be triggered, for example, by its incapacity to survive competition from other currencies. Because Bitcoin is one of the most technically vulnerable coins, this is a distinct possibility.

Trading

While many people associate trading with analysis, patterns, and technical modeling, the trader's task is a subjective judgment of market conditions.

Apart from having a glass of whiskey (grin), the first thing a competent trader should do is forecast which cryptocurrencies will grow in the market. Following that, traders must forecast the optimal entry point into the market.

What comes next?

They should continue forecasting when coin prices would begin to decrease. However, the most critical aspect of trading is having enormous expertise and even a small bit of luck. Additionally, a trader must consistently repeat all of the preceding procedures.

This is a problem, as everything rarely goes as planned, but risks must be constantly assumed.

That is why, in my opinion, trading suits those with an engineering mindset, ample time, and, most importantly, a strong spirit.

Mining

This approach requires primarily computer equipment to execute.

What comes next? You insert it into a socket and wait for the money to flow into your pocket.

What do you use the money for?

As previously stated, miners are compensated for providing computational capacity to the network. In addition, the network compensates miners with coins in exchange for their equipment and labor.

ICOs (Initial Coin Offerings)

The bitcoin market now provides additional options for active investors. This strategy is ideal if you have a lot of spare time (and money), sufficient experience, and a desire to earn large and quick gains. However, while this strategy is extremely profitable, it is also extremely hazardous, especially for novices.

The fundamental tenet of ICO strategy, which I also refer to as startups, is as follows.

The Bitcoin economy has created an incredibly simple method for individuals with unique and exciting ideas to support their endeavors. They no longer need to pound the pavement, begging and persuading large firms to invest in their idea. Instead, these innovators and developers can now post a proposal on their website. Then, if you are interested in their concept, you can publish your wallet's address to receive tokens if the concept proves successful.

The consequence is that you will have to invest money now to reap a profit later.

Historically, the regulations of ICOs were pretty straightforward.

I pay you one dollar, and you give me two tokens. Now, some initial coin offerings (ICOs) go to ludicrous lengths. In general, after investing in an ICO, you may discover that you can exchange your tokens only on Friday at midnight during the full moon and only if you are a mermaid with a blue tail. Perhaps my story is a bit exaggerated, but it exemplifies the obscurity of the regulations that govern most companies (ICOs).

If it was not difficult to locate a grain of truth amid the diversity of ICOs half a year ago (when just a handful debuted in a week and could be readily evaluated), now new ICOs occur virtually every hour, and you do not have time to evaluate them all.

What would I advise a newcomer enticed to try his luck with initial coin offerings?

To begin, you must have a thorough understanding of the industry in which you wish to invest. If you are knowledgeable about it, you can assess it and determine if it has a chance of success.

Additionally, I suggest you heed what experienced investors and professionals have to say and disregard what is mentioned on the ICO's website.

I would even argue that you should avoid investing in any initial coin offering that is not referenced in at least three professional analytical studies written by acknowledged professionals.

Penny Stocks

If you are familiar with the exchange trade, you should be familiar with the concept of penny stocks. To put it bluntly, these are shares in the company that nobody needs. However, these shares have one advantage: they are so inexpensive that nothing can prevent them from doubling in value. Such a miraculous surge can occur as a result of excellent news, a little market manipulation, or for any other reason. So, how can you put this method to work for you?

You purchase the most unusual and obscure coins and then wait to watch how the scenario develops. Throughout the year, the value of some of your coins may increase. If this occurs, you should sell this currency immediately. If you purchased fifty coins, a price increase of even one super-cheap coin would compensate for the loss of your entire investment portfolio. This strategy precludes you from delving deeply into the fundamentals of the Bitcoin business.

All you have to do is purchase 'trash' and sell it on time. However, this strategy is not within my purview because it resembles a casino. You do not require any talents or education, only good fortune. You have no control over what happens or how risks are managed because everything is contingent on good fortune.

Follow My Steps

This strategy is ideal if you lack knowledge in the bitcoin industry but have money to dabble with. However, you must be willing to accept risks and entrust your money to strangers. Because the bitcoin industry is unregulated, nobody can ensure that a corporation or someone who claimed to earn money for you would not take your money and flee to some sunny destination.

Numerous businesses on the market offer profit in exchange for trust. For example, some companies provide mining contracts to those interested in mining without investing in the necessary equipment and space. This is referred to as cloud mining.

A different form of business is cryptocurrency funds.

These companies have no idea how to mine but are adept at estimating good coins. The third category is the initial coin offering mutual funds. These people spend their time scouring the market for startups in which they will subsequently invest your money. Finally, there is trading. You cede ownership of your money to someone else, who will trade on your behalf.

After discussing these investment techniques, please understand that I do not consider these strategies perfect. Therefore, allow me to share two perfect investment strategies with you.

There are, in my opinion, two ideal strategies.

The first is based on your honest belief in the future of Bitcoin.

If this describes you, you should take on a few methods that interest you, mix them up, and begin profiting in this manner: by diversifying your possibilities of profiting as well as your risks.

If you believe in the future of the bitcoin company, you should focus on the second ideal investment strategy:

Profit from others who do.

Some people will require mining equipment and premises, some will require dollars, and still, others will require information, and you can earn money by meeting their demands.

Chapter 11. Trader Mindset

You will undoubtedly agree that the psychological mindset required to excel in any undertaking is critical. Some people are born with the appropriate mindset, while others must work to develop it.

In either case, I want to emphasize a few critical principles that can help you profit from the cryptocurrency market or, at the very least, prevent significant losses.

- **Avoid being greedy:** Do not wait for the price to increase more to profit even more. Your avarice may cost you not only profits but also a loss.

- **Maintain patience:** If you buy a currency at a specific price and do not notice significant upward or downward movement, do not panic and sell it quickly. I have witnessed numerous instances of a cryptocurrency's nearly constant price suddenly doubling in a week. You may be wondering how to avoid a loss during a market correction. My response is this: do not convert all of your cryptocurrency to fiat currency! Numerous people make this error and eventually regret it. You would be wise to check theme forums and user reviews of this coin before selling everything.

- **Always keep in mind the market's depth:** When there are a large number of sellers and a small number of buyers, you can acquire some assets at an ostensibly attractive price but fail to sell everything you have acquired.

- **Stay vigilant:** Keep an eye on the market capitalization and trading volume of a cryptocurrency.

You should follow these steps:

This is to ascertain whether spikes will be present. Thus, after analyzing cryptocurrency price fluctuations and identifying specific patterns, you can develop your strategy and trading plan. Then, you can begin refining it under real-world situations by beginning with tiny quantities that practically all transactions allow. Finally, if your method proves effective, you can increase your investments gradually.

Finally, I summarize my concise and efficient advice once more. I hope they are beneficial in assisting you in becoming a successful cryptocurrency investor.

Contrary to popular notions, do not adjust your plan at every chance. Profit from your efforts. Do not lose sight of your primary objectives. Make no rash decisions. Automate as many processes as feasible.

Conclusion

C ryptocurrency can be an unpredictable and volatile market. It is not uncommon to see the price of one currency go up or down ten, twenty, or even thirty percent in a single day. Staying informed and keeping track of the newest changes as they happen is critical if you want to participate in this market. Although many people find themselves discouraged after seeing such daily dips, these frequent highs and lows actually give crypto investors more opportunities to make gains. The volatile nature of cryptocurrency means that those who can invest during periods when coins are cheaper (sometimes hundreds of dollars) will likely see higher rewards than those who wait for the coin prices to stabilize before investing.

However, many investors will find themselves disappointed when a stock or commodity price rises to unrealistic levels and then falls back down to earth. Following the daily changes in the cryptocurrency market can help an investor identify those days when prices are rising and those days when prices are falling. For example, looking at a currency's performance over 30 days will allow an investor to notice that Bitcoin is consistently seeking new highs while many other cryptos are experiencing volatility. This information can also help an investor detect changes in sentiment. If a coin is being pumped or dumped by bots or other traders, this may be a sign that people are taking a more serious interest in the coin's value.

When investing in cryptocurrency, an investor is going to be limited by the supply of available coins. The market cap of anyone cryptocurrency is always going to be small compared to the value of all cryptocurrencies combined. When prices are rising, this means that prices for large amounts of coins will also rise. So, if a currency has a daily trading volume and a high number of transactions being made on its network, this might indicate that the coin has a lot more potential in the future than others without those features.

Glossary

- **Bitcoin:** Bitcoin was the first currency to be invented in the digital age. It's a currency that can be used to buy and sell products and services without interference from a third party, like a bank or credit card company because transactions are made directly from person to person. And while traditional currencies rely on physical coins and paper money, bitcoins transactions are based on public-key cryptography. The genius behind it all is Satoshi Nakamoto who published this article about bitcoin's design—then went mysteriously silent as bitcoin began to gain traction as an alternative currency.

- **Blockchain:** Blockchain is an online ledger of sorts, storing data about transactions between users. Your involvement with blockchain generally depends on what type of user you are. If you're not familiar with blockchain, or what it does exactly, here's some information to get you up to speed.

- **Broker:** A Broker is an individual or organization that brings together disparate parties to buy and sell stocks, bonds, commodities, real estate, etc. While the term 'broker' is used in various fields to refer to individuals or organizations that provide brokerage services (that is buying and selling for others) this article only deals with stockbrokers.

- **Cryptocurrency:** Cryptocurrencies are digital assets that have become an economic phenomenon in the last few years. These assets use cryptography to protect transactions and control the creation of new units in a process referred to as mining. The creation of new units is typically restricted in time or quantity or both. It uses decentralized systems that regulate transactions without any central authority managing your funds for you.

- **Currency:** Currency is an economic system in which the medium of exchange, usually a piece or pieces of paper or metal, has a value that can be exchanged for goods and services within a country or across borders.

- **DEFI:** The term DEFI is used to describe a Decentralized Finance. It's a generalization of the decentralized crypto-space that can be used to describe the state of crypto in general, or just remind yourself of what DEFI stands for.

- **Ethereum:** Ethereum is a decentralized platform that runs smart contracts, which are autonomous scripts that run on the blockchain. The most interesting thing about Ethereum is how many different applications it can be used for.

- **NFT**: NFT stands for Non-Fungible Token. It is a type of cryptocurrency. Different types of NFTs have been written about on the internet and you can use these to create digital assets in a game, establish ownership over an economic system, or make other digital objects within your application.

- **NFT Art:** NFT Art in Crypto is the design and implementation of artwork that exists on the Ethereum blockchain. Here you will find a detailed guide for new artists, including an explanation about cryptocurrency vs art, and how to create your own NFT artwork.

- **Trader:** A trader is a person who buys and sells securities, commodities, or foreign currencies in an attempt to make a profit on the difference between the prices. In other words, this investment strategy focuses on buying low and selling high.

- **Trading:** Trading is a financial transaction where two parties agree to exchange goods of equivalent value on some terms. In the most common form, one party provides the other with something of value (usually money) and then takes back another that it wants or needs. The 'first party' is said to be the seller, and the 'second party' is said to be the buyer. The 'first party' is typically called the seller, and the 'second party' is called the buyer when they are acting jointly.

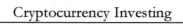

CPSIA information can be obtained
at www.ICGtesting.com
Printed in the USA
BVHW052018100223
658274BV00001B/273